Rotterdam invasion of Holland

Wilhelmina Steenbeek

BB

Editor-in-Chief: Barrie Pitt
Editor: David Mason
Art Director: Sarah Kingham
Picture Editor: Robert Hunt
Designer: David Allen
Cover: Denis Piper
Special Drawings: John Batchelor
Photographic Research: Carina Dvorak
Cartographer: Richard Natkiel
Translated by Charlotte Mayer

Contents

A city destroyed

Introduction by Sydney L Mayer

The Netherlands lived behind a wall of neutrality for over a century. Born during the Eighty Years War, it had endured war with a series of enemies throughout most of its early history. By successfully resisting Imperial Spain, against enormous odds, it ultimately won its independence. This independence, and the wealth of a new colonial empire which came in its wake, had to be stoutly defended in a number of wars against many enemies, sometimes Spain again, in combination with others, then England, and then France. Always the Dutch resisted, and if they did not always win, at least their independence and access to the outside world through sea power was maintained. But two centuries and more of war proved debilitating, and the conquest of Holland during the French Revolution destroyed the myth that Holland was indestructible. A shadowy independence was maintained at first as a puppet of the French, to begin with as a republic – later as a monarchy under Napoleon's brother – but finally all pretence was dropped: in 1811 Holland was absorbed directly into the Napoleonic Empire. When the Empire fell and Holland was liberated, the Nether-lands, now swelled by the addition of Belgium and Luxembourg, gave up all aspirations to becoming a great power, and was content to act as a prosperous buffer state between a resurgent Prussia and France.

The secession of Belgium from the union in 1830 proved a mixed blessing but, like Belgium itself, this reduced Dutch state hoped to solve its international status by opting for neutrality. As the wars of German and Italian unification upset the European balance of power in the 19th century, the Netherlands stood aloof, bourgeois, conservative and, above all, safe from foreign intervention. Although the First World War proved to the Belgians that neutrality provided no adequate defence against a ruthless invader, the Dutch were lucky enough to avoid conflict. They sold goods to both sides and profited thereby, only suffering certain deprivations when the British blockade of the Continent became more effective in the last eighteen months of the war. Little was provided in the way of defence. It was too costly, it was argued, and unnecessary. Had not war been avoided without costly expenditure? The fate of Belgium, occupied and ravaged for four years, had had little impact on Dutch attitudes, even though many Dutchmen could see and hear the war going on from the safety of their living rooms if they lived close enough to the Belgian border.

Throughout the 1920s Germany was pliant, militarily weak, and wracked with unemployment and inflation, and only a minute fraction of the Dutch budget was spent on defence. When Hitler came to power, although the danger to Holland's safety was obvious, little more was spent on defence than in the 1920s. There was an unwritten, almost unspoken, assumption that if war came to Europe again Holland could somehow remain aloof, safe in her neutrality, as she had done before. This illusion was smashed on 10th May 1940, when waves of planes dropped their bombs and parachutists descended on a state which was not only militarily but psychologically unprepared for war. As in other Western democracies, the voices of reason which called repeatedly for rearmament and alliance with her natural allies, Britain and France, went unheeded. The destruction of one of her greatest cities, Rotterdam, was an even greater shock than the invasion itself. In five days the independence of the Netherlands was destroyed. Rotterdam, which the Germans bombed by mistake, lay in ruins, along with Holland's neutralist policy.

Wilhelmina Steenbeek, who lived through this holocaust of war and occupation, describes the invasion of her unprepared fatherland and the horrors of the bombing of her native city. No Dutchman who lived through the Second World War can ever forget the sudden violence of the *blitzkrieg* or the wanton, needless destruction of one of its greatest cities. Out of the ashes of war, a new Rotterdam and a new Holland have risen, but the lessons of the war have been dearly bought. It is unlikely that the Dutch people will ever return to an ostrich-like posture of neutralism, which provides no adequate defence against the predatory aggressor.

The German bombs destroyed the heart of a great city, but nothing could destroy the hearts of its people. Rotterdam Redux lives on. Its great spiritual heart rebuilt Rotterdam from the rubble of war, a symbol of a renascent Netherlands and Europe.

Fool's paradise

Tourists visiting Rotterdam admire Zadkine's powerful sculpture of a man extending his arms towards the sky. Ordinary visitors see it merely as a piece of 'modern art' – the figure of a man with a gaping hole in his body. They are not aware that this hole symbolises the condition of the city of Rotterdam itself, a city still beautiful in a modern way, and struggling upwards in search of material success, but from which the heart has been torn away. During the day the town is the picture of vivacity: the bustling harbours, the energetic hard working people, the cacophony of the corn exchange building, the busy shoppers in the Lijnbaan – a well-known shopping centre; it all has a stimulating effect on the visitor, but at night all is quiet. The people of Rotterdam work in their town, but for the most part they do not live or have their recreation there; the magnificent theatre stands almost empty. For pleasure they often go to nearby Breda, or even Antwerp in Belgium, which is really not too far away.

Before 1940, however, Rotterdam had an exciting night life and was a focus of culture. The picturesque centre with its old monuments, large library and numerous art treasures attracted people from miles around. Its cinemas and theatres were crowded nightly, and the Schiedamse Dijk, known to sailors all over the world, was alive with the music coming out of its little cafés and the sights and smells of a rich and vital city. But that city, the Rotterdam where I was born, is gone.

In 1940 Rotterdam was planning to celebrate the sixth centenary of the official existence of the town, having been granted city rights in 1340. From that time the town grew steadily, and thanks to its favourable location it became an important commercial centre, where many German and British immigrants came to settle. Antwerp, its great rival, outdid Rotterdam until 1847, when the Nieuwe Waterweg, a canal connecting Rotterdam with the North Sea, was opened. From then on its prosperity grew, and the people of Rotterdam confirmed their reputation for hard work, displaying imagination, energy and foresight. But the growing prosperity also attracted more people than the town could comfortably hold, and this was especially so in the centre of the city. Notwithstanding its marvellous atmosphere and vitality, poor families were cramped in houses too small for them, without adequate sanitary arrangements, and it was there that, in May 1940, the bombs fell. A mistake made by the Luftwaffe caused 80,000 people in Rotterdam, approximately thirteen per cent of the population, to lose their homes. More than 2,500 shops were demolished. One hundred of these were small shops which sold hot water (*waterstokerijen*). These were a typical feature of the city's poor neighbourhoods where the people had to purchase hot water in order to wash their laundry, and serve other necessities of life, being without any hot water supply of their own. About 500 cafés were destroyed, including those on the Schiedamse Dijk, and almost 70 schools together with 21 churches, 12 cinemas, 20 large bank buildings, 4 hospitals and 2 theatres. Irreplacable art treasures, especially those held privately, went up in flames. The intellectual world lost its great library, the Rotterdam *Leeskabinet*, one of the greatest in Holland. The Church of St Lawrence, built in the 15th century, was also destroyed leaving only a shell, though the structure was restored after the war at enormous cost with money raised from private funds. The Church of St Rosalie, Rotterdam's incomparable rococo monument, which had been restored only a few years before the Second World War, was demolished along with the synagogue built in 1725 on the Boompjes, once a lovely tree-lined *quai*.

'May 1940 – Destroyed City'; Zadkine's sculpture reminds Rotterdamers of the destruction of their town

9

The great bridges of the wealthy city in 1934, prime goals of the German invaders six years later

The events preceding this disaster are of significance with regard to policies of comfortable neutrality. The example of Rotterdam will remain always as a chilling reminder of the consequences of unpreparedness.

Why, then, was Holland so ill-prepared for an obviously inescapable war? The training of troops was almost non-existent, weapons were old-fashioned (the Dutch army used rifles which dated as far back as 1890) and for transport some battalions had only bicycles. The principal culprit was a general and quite unfounded optimism, prompted by an unwillingness to face reality, that Germany would honour Holland's neutrality. The order for general mobilization did not come through until 29th August 1939.

After the *Anschluss* of Austria and part of Czechoslovakia, Hitler embarked on the invasion of Poland. This event at last caused England and France to declare war on Germany, on 3rd September 1939 – an inevitable but still courageous step, considering the military strength of the enemy. Germany had mobilized 105 divisions. Fifty-nine of these were fighting in Poland, but behind the *Westwall* forty-three divisions were ready to attack the West-European countries. On the face of it France could easily counterattack with her eighty-four divisions, but these consisted mainly of troops trained for defence and therefore not in a state of readiness for aggressive action. Britain was in more or less the same position, only recently having begun to build up her army. According to the London War Office more than 1,600 tanks were needed and only sixty were at hand. Germany possessed approximately the

Rotterdam's busy harbours, key to her mercantile prosperity, in the early 1930s

11

**Antique field guns of the Dutch army.
Much of the equipment of the armed
forces was of this vintage**

same number of aircraft as France and
Britain together, but the German
machines were modern and efficient
whereas the Allied planes were in the
main hopelessly old-fashioned and
decrepit. Only in sea power did the
Allies have obvious superiority.

British and French confidence in
their navies was the chief reason for
Germany being allowed so much time
to prepare for war by building up an
adequately armed and well trained
army and air force. Both Chamberlain
and Daladier had been of the opinion
that, with the help of their colonies
and the British Dominions, and – if it
became necessary – of the Americans,
Germany could be brought to her
knees by means of a blockade. They
were in no hurry to enter a war. And
anyway one could not possibly believe
that Hitler would try to conquer the
whole of Western Europe. Compound-
ing these delusions, the French had an
incurable faith in their Maginot Line
which, we must mention, extended no
further than Belgium. Up to the
middle of December Britain's Prime
Minister still did not believe that
Germany had any intention of attacking the West; General Montgomery
retorted that Hitler would start a big
offensive in Western Europe just as
soon as he saw fit. In reality the offensive had already been put off several
times because of bad weather.

It was Hitler's repeated postponement of the date of the German attack
which caused the Dutch government
to disbelieve the warnings of Major
G J Sas, the Dutch Military Attaché
at the Embassy in Berlin. He had a
good friend there, Colonel Hans Oster,
a German regular officer, and these
two men had known each other well

**A Dutch civil defence unit before the
Second World War. These men had at
least some training, unlike all too many
of the troops thrown into battle in 1940**

for years and trusted each other. Oster had been in service during the First World War, was a royalist, and had a great liking for the Netherlands, where the German Emperor had found asylum in 1919. He told Sas that he did not believe in Mr Hitler's National Socialism. He dreaded a second world war and he had fought the Nazi movement since its foundation. (He was hanged at Floosenburg in April 1945 after the unsuccessful attempt to kill Hitler on 20th July 1944.) He was well informed since he worked at the agency for the compilation of military intelligence and subsequently was appointed head of the *Zentralabteilung,* where his position kept him in contact with the various military attachés in Berlin. All the information he gave Sas proved later to be true. He warned him, for instance, that the members of the Royal Family should take care for their security, that the bridges over the Maas would be blown up sooner or later, that the Germans would use airborne troops and tanks and that some of the German troops would be dressed in Dutch uniforms. Towards the end of January 1940 he revealed that a complete tank division would invade Rotterdam via Noord-Brabant (a province in the south of the Netherlands, adjoining Belgium), the bridges at the Moerdijk and the bridge at Dordrecht. This last report, perhaps the most important one, went astray. General Winkelman, General Reynders' successor as C-in-C army and navy, never saw it.

On 12th September 1939 Hitler told his generals that he intended to attack the West as soon as Poland surrendered. A great many of the generals thought the plan foolhardy, maintaining that the German army did not

The Dutch army receives new blood. The carefree mood evident was soon shattered

15

An assembly point during the general mobilisation of August 1939

Major G J Sas, Military Attaché at the Dutch Embassy in Berlin, repeatedly warned his superiors of the imminent German attack but was consistently disbelieved

General Winkelman, Commander in Chief from January 1940, saw the military situation more clearly than his predecessor General Reynders

General Brauchitsch in 1940. The
general acted as spokesman for the
Führer's military advisers,
recommending postponement of the
offensive in the West. His advice was
declined

have enough trucks and that the ammunition available would not be sufficient for more than one third of the divisions at that time ready for battle, and then for no more than two weeks of action. Hitler swept these objections aside. Even if the *Wehrmacht* was weak, the French and British were weaker still. On 8th October he dictated a message to be sent to General Keitel, head of the *Oberkommando der Wehrmacht*, and the commanders-in-chief of army, navy and air force: General von Brauchitsch, Admiral Raeder and *Generalfeldmarschall* Göring respectively. He informed them of the importance of defeating France and Britain as soon as possible, and made clear his unfavourable assessment of the Soviet Union as an ally. The Ruhr Valley, of vital importance to Germany's war industry, must be safeguarded, and if Holland and Belgium yielded to the persuasion of France and Britain and abandoned their neutrality the Ruhr Valley would be in danger. Since

Hitler broods over his plans before
the invasion of Holland; Brauchitsch,
army C-in-C, on his right

The Minister for Foreign Affairs, van Kleffens. The British Ambassador at the Hague notified him of Hitler's intention to invade, supplementing Major Sas's warnings

General I H Reynders, Commander in Chief of the Dutch Army and Navy, who did his best to discredit Sas. His replacement by General Winkelman came not a moment too soon

attack is the best form of defence, it would be advisable to invade the neutral countries as soon as possible. An added advantage would be the securing for Germany of the coasts of Holland and Belgium, and perhaps the Channel coast, for air bases, making Britain an easier target.

Hitler also envisaged the possibility that the Allies might occupy Belgium themselves, another reason for the German troops to attack immediately. The Führer and his generals therefore planned a huge offensive, code named *Fall Gelb* (Case Yellow), the first version of which was ready on 19th October. The theatre of operations was to be principally Belgium, since in the event of a German attack the French and British armies could penetrate Belgium from the south. In the first version priority was given to overwhelming Utrecht, Amsterdam and Rotterdam. This scheme was replaced by another in which more troops would be concentrated in the south. Only the German Sixth Army would cross the south of the Netherlands on their way to Brussels, in which case *Vesting Holland* (Fortress Holland) would remain intact. The date set for *Fall Gelb* was 12th November 1939.

The generals were still not very enthusiastic; most divisions were not ready for combat, much necessary material was lacking and training and organisation needed to be perfected. Brauchitsch volunteered to advise Hitler that it was most undesirable to attack so soon, but a very irritated Führer rejected the criticisms out of hand and personally gave the order to start the preparations for 'Case Yellow'. The troops moved towards the borders of Holland, Belgium and Luxembourg on the night of 5th November. The army whose route lay through Luxembourg had orders to prepare its right flank to repel possible Dutch attacks because, although it was well known that the Dutch divisions were not a real danger, any delay however short could be fatal. For what was to prevent the Dutch from blowing up the bridges over the Maas and the Belgians the bridges over the Albert Canal? Hitler was extremely concerned about this possibility and attempted to secure his avenues of advance by means of a complex plan involving the placing of German soldiers in Dutch and Belgian uniforms at strategic points. But where to find the uniforms? A great number were needed, not only army uniforms but also those of customs officials, police, railway workers and so on. The Generals were in fact unaware that some Dutch uniforms were actually manufactured in Germany, and also that old uniforms were sold as rags to Germany, so an attempt was made to buy the necessary garments in Holland. A German officer, having some friends in Holland who were members of the NSB (*National Socialistische Bond* or National Socialist Union), undertook to acquire the uniforms which were needed. However, a Jewish shop-keeper in Amsterdam, who traded in second-hand clothes, became suspicious, noted the number of the licence plate of the car in which the uniforms were collected, and called the police. The car was stopped at the border, the owner was arrested, the uniforms were confiscated and the whole plot fell through. But amazingly enough nobody apparently drew the obvious conclusions from the circumstance of Germans wishing to purchase Dutch uniforms. The Dutch Railways organization ordered all its employees to carry identity cards after the incident, but that was all. The German officer involved, Gerken, escaped and so could not be questioned. Subsequently, on 12th May, two days after the Dutch capitulation, he returned to free his Dutch accomplices, then imprisoned in Almelo; he compelled the prison governor to release them and then destroyed all the documents relating to the operation.

On Saturday 4th November the British Ambassador at The Hague, Sir Neville Bland, informed the Dutch Minister for Foreign Affairs, van Kleffens, that Germany would attack Holland and Belgium on 12th November. The Queen was informed, as was General Reynders. The general did not think it necessary to pass the message to Sas in Berlin; he did not trust the Military Attaché overmuch, considering him one of those tiresome people who love to make others feel uneasy with stories of impending doom. Sas, however, knew already that Germany was training airborne troops and paratroopers and that German soldiers in Polish uniforms would be used in the attack on Poland. After the fall of Poland he knew quite well that the West would be the next target. His warnings were all but ignored in The Hague, and the suspicion that he was 'crying wolf' was increased because he never mentioned the name of his principal informant, Oster, but always referred to him as 'a German Officer'.

The Dutch cabinet as a whole, at that time a decorative body consisting

largely of the half senile and inert, considered Sas, who was quite an emotional man, an extravagant character and therefore very untrustworthy. They decided to send an ex-officer, Lieutenant-Colonel Gijsberti Hodenpijl, who had been Military Attaché in Berlin during the First World War, to Germany to see how much truth, if any, there was in Sas's allegations. Hodenpijl visited all his old buddies in Berlin and was assured that they knew nothing about an impending attack on Holland, so, quite satisfied, he returned a comforting message to The Hague: nothing was wrong. It so happened that a friend of Sas was at the Department when that report arrived. He was so shocked by it that he called Sas who came immediately to The Hague, to the great disapproval of General Reynders. The General, Commander-in-Chief of Army and Navy, told him in so many words that he did not wish Sas to have direct contact with Dijxhoorn (Minister of Defence) nor with van Kleffens (Minister for Foreign Affairs) but only and solely with him, the General. Deeply disillusioned, Sas returned to Berlin.

Despite official disbelief in Sas, however, some apprehension of danger was penetrating. The Dutch generals decided to inundate the defence line at the Grebbe and partly close the roads to and from the border. Minister van Kleffens proposed that the Queen, together with the King of Belgium, should appeal to Germany, France and Britain to make an end to the war. The Queen thought this to be an excellent idea and the same evening wrote a letter to 'Mon cher Léopold' containing the proposal to send telegrams to Hitler, King George VI and President Lebrun. Unfortunately Hitler refused to cooperate. Nevertheless the Dutch remained optimistic; on 9th November one could read in the newspapers: 'Our government sees no reason for alarm'.

The day before an attempt had been made to kill Hitler in the Bürgerbraukeller in Munich (the *Bierputsch*), and Minister van Kleffens had declared in Parliament: 'The Germans could invade us tomorrow'.

On 20th January 1940 Churchill, in a broadcast, reproached the small neutral powers, asserting that they were waiting, trembling with fright, to see which of them would be devoured first, hoping against hope that the storm would pass before it was their turn. If only they were willing to cooperate, the danger could be avoided, he said. In Holland this did not have the result Churchill hoped for. In the view of the neutral countries, Britain and France had no right to impose their wishes on them, especially since in the recent past they had not helped any of the nations overwhelmed by Germany and Russia. One had only to look at the examples of Poland, Czechoslovakia and Finland. Finland had applied for help to the League of Nations and the only effect was Russia's expulsion from the League, which helped the Finns not at all; no aid was offered, and after three months of tough and heroic combat the Finns were forced to capitulate. The concensus view in the Netherlands was that if they declared for the Allies that action alone would cause the Germans to invade immediately. At all costs this had to be prevented. It was held that only strict neutrality would save the Netherlands, as it had in the First World War. That history might not repeat itself in this respect was an idea difficult to comprehend for most Dutch people. They did not suspect or, if they were suspicious, preferred not to believe, that Hitler planned to attack the Netherlands. In fact he wanted only a pretext, an excuse. That excuse he got by way of the Venlo Incident, an affair hardly mentioned in the Dutch press, and of which therefore the Dutch themselves remained almost totally ignorant.

Winston Churchill in early 1940.
The neutral countries reacted
sceptically to his call for solidarity
to deter Hitler

Venlo
and
violation

A German communications post in a Copenhagen street. The drive into Scandinavia clearly demonstrated the Nazi attitude to neutrals

in 1938. Koutrik had acquired a great deal of knowledge, and through him the Germans learned all the names and addresses of the British Secret Service agents. The head of the Dutch Secret Service was Major-General van Oorschot who, though on at least superficially good terms with the German Military Attachés, in fact was an anglophile; he had seen the inevitability of a second world war for many years.

Officially van Oorschot had no contact whatsoever with the British Secret Service – the Dutch Government would not have approved – but in fact there was close cooperation between the various secret services of the Netherlands, Great Britain and France, and all intelligence gathered about the *Wehrmacht* was circulated among them, liaison being accomplished by a Dutch reporter. The Czech Intelligence Service later became part of this association, one of their contacts being a German named Thümmel who warned them about the offensive against Poland; he was arrested in 1942 and eventually executed in the Theresienstadt camp in April 1945.

All information received by the Secret Service was carefully scrutinized and double-checked where possible, as German counter-intelligence was in the habit of planting false information – so-called *Spielmaterial*. In fact, everybody did the same and with considerable success, making it very difficult to determine which information was true and which false. The same applied to the informants; one never knew for certain that they were genuine. Many members of the German Secret Service in the Netherlands posed as political fugitives, and often enough they succeeded in fooling the Dutch. One such was Dr Franz Fischer, who succeeded in contacting

In the Netherlands the British Secret Service operated in the guise of the 'Passport Control Office', founded in The Hague during the First World War. The head of the operation, Major R H Stevens, whose task mainly consisted of compiling intelligence about the German army, was supplied with information by Dutchmen who travelled regularly to Germany. His intermediary was a man called Vrinten whose activities, unfortunately, were no mystery to the Germans, as one of Vrinten's partners, Friedrich Günther, had long been a German double agent who reported to the *Abwehr* in Hamburg. Another of Vrinten's partners, Koutrik, also went over to the *Abwehr*

Major-General van Oorschot for whom the Venlo Incident spelled the end of a career as head of the Dutch Secret Service

The Dutch Minister of Defence, Dijxhoorn. Neither he nor van Kleffens were informed of the Venlo manoeuvrings

Captain S Payne Best, appointed agent of British Intelligence in the Hague, and deceived by the German *agents provocateurs*

Walter Schellenberg, alias Hauptmann Schemmel of the 'Opposition to Hitler' key figure of the Venlo Incident

a Dr Spiecker in London. Dr Spiecker had been the head of the Press office of the *Reichskanzlei*, and was particularly interested in disillusioned and dissatisfied German officers, under which disguise Fischer gave him much false information which was passed to the other Secret Services via the British Intelligence Service. Fischer's superior was a certain Dr Solms, and they were able to play their game for a full eight months before they aroused the suspicion of the head of the Passport Control Office, at that time Major Chidson. He broke all contact with them but presumably did not inform his successor, Major Stevens, nor London Headquarters. A curious oversight.

The Passport Control Office were unaware that the British Intelligence Service had another agent in The Hague (whereas the Germans probably knew the real function of the Passport Control Office), so Captain S Payne Best, who was married to a Dutch wife and had been living in The Hague for some years, was appointed. Spiecker instructed Fischer to contact Payne Best, who was briefed by London Headquarters to meet Dr Solms with Fischer as the middleman. Payne Best communicated with London via Stevens of the Passport Control Office. Payne Best met Solms in Venlo during the second half of September 1939, and was told a story about a plot to eliminate Hitler. Solms did not know all the details but the leaders of the plot would try soon enough to get in touch with Payne Best and give him more information. After that one meeting Solms did not appear again, the pretext being that the Gestapo was suspicious and therefore he had to stay under cover; Reinhard Heydrich, Secret Police Chief, had decided to replace Solms by two SS Officers who, for the purpose of the deception in hand, were called *Leutnant* Grosch and *Hauptmann* von Seidlitz. In the meantime Payne Best had informed the Dutch Intelligence Service about his contacts with the

German 'resistance', and the Dutch in turn sent one Lieutenant Klop whose job was to listen and report everything to General Reynders. Ministers Dijxhoorn and van Kleffens were kept in the dark. The first meeting took place near Dinxperlo at the Dutch-German border on 21st October, Klop calling himself 'Copper' and claiming to be an Englishman – not difficult for him since he had lived in Canada and was fluent in the English language. The German party said that they could not stay long as they had to be back before 8 o'clock, and it was agreed that the first talk would take place in Arnhem. In Arnhem they were almost arrested because a waiter became suspicious. Not much was learned from this talk and the English were very disappointed, but they hoped to meet more important members of the 'opposition to Hitler' at the next meeting. That took place on 30th October when Best and Stevens met 'three members of the plot'. In place of *Hauptmann* von Seidlitz came Walter Schellenberg, under the alias of '*Hauptmann* Schemmel', a promising pupil of the SD *Hauptamt*, though still too young for the part of 'General'. The Austrian professor de Croms went to Holland under the name of 'Colonel Martini' as 'the leader of the opposition's' right hand man. He and '*Leutnant* Grosch' were arrested near Arnhem, but Klop managed to get them freed. During the talk they detailed the German losses during the Polish campaign, and emphasized that it was of vital importance that the war end immediately. But before they could take action they would need to know the terms for peace to which France and Britain would agree. Payne Best relayed the information to Lord Halifax, the British Minister for Foreign Affairs, whose reaction to the news was fairly cool; nevertheless he thought it worthwhile to proceed with the contacts.

On 7th November they met for the third time. The Germans, disliking Venlo as a meeting place, suggested a

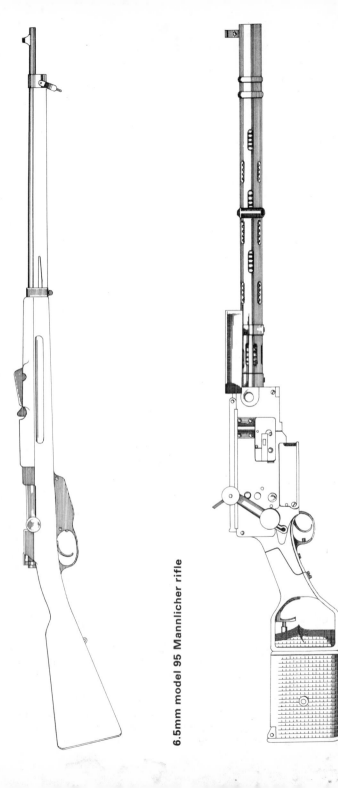

6.5mm model 95 Mannlicher rifle

Madsen M1929 light machine-gun – calibre 6.5mm: This is typical of the many models of Madsen machine-guns designed by the famous Danish firm, which were used, with various types of mounts, by the Netherlands armed forces

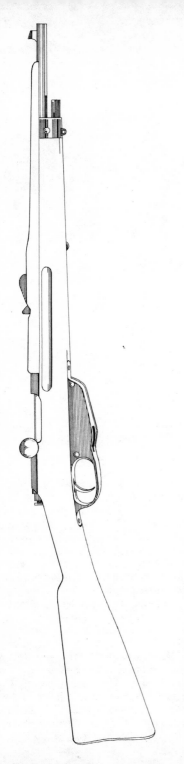

6.5mm model 95, No. 3 NM Mannlicher carbine

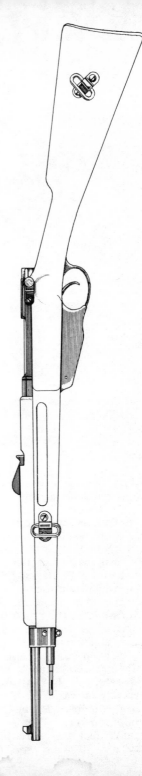

6.5mm model 95, No. 4 NM Mannlicher carbine

Part of the Dutch army under inspection before their barracks

Dutch café, the 'Backus', only about five yards from the border. There 'Schemmel' apologized for the absence of the General, who regretted very much not being able to attend the meeting but who would come next day and personally hand them most important documents. On the 8th the General was still unable to come, since Hitler had summoned all his generals to a meeting to discuss Queen Wilhelmina and King Leopold's peace proposals; but the day after he would certainly appear.

On 9th November Payne Best, Stevens and Klop went to Venlo. They had begun to feel less sure of the situation and went armed. Klop told them that Headquarters had received information that the German invasion of Holland could be expected at any moment, which disturbing news – though they did not really believe it – made them ill at ease. On arrival at Venlo Klop went to the *Koninklijke Marechaussee* (State Police) to ask them to send a patrol to the Backus as a security measure, and while they made their way by car two *Marechaussees* followed by bicycle. At the border post Klop left the car to tell the customs official that they were going to the Backus, the others meanwhile parking the car near the café. No sooner had they done this than a German military car stormed round a corner with Germans hanging out at

and revealed his true identity – SS officer Schellenberg. He sent them to Berlin to be interrogated by a specialist on the British Secret Intelligence Service. Payne Best refused to tell anything but Stevens, who was carrying a list of names, was more forthcoming, and Lemmens, the chauffeur, confirmed the story. Lemmens was set free in November 1940, but Payne Best and Stevens had to spend the rest of the war in Dachau concentration camp where fortunately Stevens was treated quite well, even being allowed to go to the theatre in Munich accompanied by a guard.

German Intelligence now had more reason to suspect close cooperation between the British and Dutch Secret Services, but still had nothing concrete. It was clear that for its part the Dutch Government did not know just how warm were relations among the various Intelligence Services and they even insisted on a thorough investigation; the Germans did not react, for of course they could not afford to have the matter investigated.

Klop's signature, appearing on his papers, was in fact the most valuable weapon found by the Germans. Expertly faked, it authenticated a fantastic story of Dutch perfidy which served to excuse the invasion of the Netherlands.

In the meantime the date of *Fall Gelb* had been fixed for the 12th of November. Oster warned Sas, who immediately went to The Hague. But because of bad weather *Fall Gelb* was put back to 15th November, and news of the postponement came through too late for Oster to get in touch with Sas. Sas did not know either that the British Ambassador in the Netherlands, Sir Neville Bland, had also warned the Dutch Government of the imminent invasion. In The Hague Sas received a very lukewarm reception, and being a man of quite emotional character, was infuriated by the lethargy of the ministers. Beside himself with anger he shouted that he would go direct to the Queen. General

both sides and firing off revolvers, in the best Chicago gangster tradition. Best and Stevens did not have time even to draw their guns. Klop tried to fire but a bullet went through his head (he died on the way to the Düsseldorf Hospital). Stevens and Best, and their driver Lemmens, were handcuffed and transported to Gestapo Headquarters. When the two bicycling policemen of the *Marechaussee* arrived at 'Café Backus' everything was over.

The Dutch government was not happy about the outcome of the exercise, and General van Oorschot, Head of the Dutch Secret Service, was required to resign.

It was useless for Payne Best and Stevens to pretend that they were innocent; 'Schemmel' knew better

The writing on the wall; Denmark and Norway are invaded. A detachment of German troops hauls a field gun through the dunes on Denmark's North Sea coast.

Reynders, whose attitude to Sas we have already discussed, took it upon himself to send a message to the Queen's adjutant, and Sas found the door closed. On the next day Minister Dijxhoorn interviewed Sas and forbade him to ask for an audience with the Queen, although by this time Sas's anger had subsided somewhat, partly due to his discovery that the information he had brought was substantiated by Sir Neville Bland's warnings, and that at least some action was about to be taken.

All army leave was cancelled, a long overdue move, but only on 11th November was the Netherlands Bank informed of the danger. A director went post-haste to The Hague and learned from Sas that there was only a slight chance that the Germans would not invade that same night. After he had conferred with Trip, the President of the Netherlands Bank, two ships of the *Maatschappij Zeeland* were immediately chartered and, during the night of 19th-20th November, were loaded with gold–166 million Dutch Guilders. (When the attack failed to materialize, the gold stayed where it was, packed in its little wooden boxes.)

General Reynders declared complete readiness of the troops at the border and of the air force; but of course *Fall Gelb* had been postponed again because of the weather, and indeed postponements for this reason – no less than nineteen in all – went on up to 10th May 1940.

The Prime Minister, de Geer, gave a reassuring broadcast: there was no reason whatever for fear ... one should not believe the news in the foreign papers.

Hitler seized on this for his

propaganda, according to which rumours of a German invasion were merely the low intrigues of Britain and France whose purpose was to persuade the neutral countries to side against Germany. The Dutch press praised Minister de Geer, declaring him to be one of the few to keep cool in the midst of frenzied warmongers.

The Dutch army leaders began to lose faith in the government and the general public to nurse unfounded hopes for a peaceful future.

Sas's fight to get his warnings across began to look ever more hopeless, especially when General Reynders was told that all his information came from an officer of the *Abwehr*. He was certain that this could not be so; according to Reynders it was utterly incredible that a German officer would be so regardless of his honour as to turn traitor. And of course each time Sas gave a new invasion date and no invasion occurred his conviction that Sas was a troublesome neurotic deepened. Initially the Dutch Embassy in Berlin did not believe Sas's information to be genuine either, but later intelligence from other sources caused them to change their minds. Gerbrandy, the Dutch Ambassador in Berlin, and the Queen were almost the only people of importance who did not consider Sas to be a complete idiot; Reynders even gave orders that the information Sas sent should be conveyed neither to the Queen, because it would make her nervous, nor to Minister Dijxhoorn, because he would start interfering with the army, which General Reynders would not like at all. The Queen, however, had asked Sas to send copies of his reports direct to one of her adjutants, from whom they would reach her. Later she explained confidentially that she could well understand people being upset by Sas's flamboyant manner, but that the politicians should have been able to discount his personal quirks and recognize the truth notwithstanding.

Relations between the army and government became considerably better when, at the end of January 1940, Reynders was succeeded by General Winkelman, at that time sixty-three years old. New tactics were planned and the general obtained all the money he wanted for his proposed measures.

In the previous November General Reynders had sent memos, at the instigation of Minister van Kleffens, to the Embassies in Brussels, Paris and London, to be read only in the event of Germany invading the Netherlands. Towards the end of March General Winkelman added new memos in which he asked for the help of the French and of the Royal Air Force if Germany attacked Holland. Some units of the Dutch navy had sealed envelopes aboard containing special charts, evacuation routes to England, and the recognition code of the Royal Navy. Plans were completed for the gold of the Netherlands Bank, all this time packed in its small cases aboard the two chartered vessels, to be escorted across the North Sea by British destroyers; and a direct radio link was established between the Chief of Staff of the Dutch navy in The Hague and the Admiralty in London. These precautions proved later to be of enormous help in the preparations for the evacuation of the Royal Family and the Government.

On 9th April 1940 the German forces not only invaded Denmark but Oslo and all the Norwegian harbours up to Narvik. Hitler had assured for Germany the iron ore of North Sweden, exported via Narvik. Colonel Oster had informed Sas about the impending attacks six days earlier; Sas had passed the intelligence on to the Danish naval attaché – whose government did not believe him – and to the Norwegian Chancellor – who thought fit not to inform his government. The whole operation cost the *Kriegmarine* no more than three cruisers, ten destroyers and one submarine.

On 19th April the Dutch government proclaimed martial law throughout

...ous advance in Norway's testing ...in. Officials in both countries had failed to act on Sas's explicit warnings

the country. This meant, among other things, that the 30,000 members of the NSB (the Dutch National Socialist Movement) had to be kept under constant surveillance and that the press was now censored. The number 30,000 referred only to registered members of the NSB; in addition there were not a few who sympathised without actually becoming formal members. (These avoided trouble later, though many had been active enough, by dis-

votes. The NSB programme – the abolition of all other political parties, the elimination of parliament, the prohibition of strikes and the institution of forced labour – was, of course, disguised somewhat for the purpose of electioneering, but became sufficiently clear later and caused many to resign in the years immediately preceding the war. Indeed by 1937 membership was little more than half the 1935 figure. Nevertheless many NSB

Near Oslo German officers confer in front of a Gloster Gladiator, late of the Norwegian air force

claiming any connection with the Movement.) In 1935 the membership had been much more extensive. During that time of widespread unemployment NSB candidates stood for election in the provincial government with the slogan 'One People', and obtained almost eight per cent of the

members kept paying their fees out of a misplaced loyalty, or rather obstinacy (a national characteristic), for which they were to pay dearly later on.

Fall Gelb had again been reorganised. Now, not only the south but the whole of the Netherlands was to be captured in one go, to withdraw Dutch territory, the plan stated, from the grip of Britain. The Netherlands unoccupied would be a weak point in Germany's defensive perimeter. As Dr L de Jong remarks in his *Het Koninkrijk der Nederlanden in de Tweede Wereldoorlog* (The Kingdom of the Netherlands during the Second World War): 'The Allied forces could penetrate from Holland straight into the Ruhr territory and paralyse Germany's war apparatus. This had to be prevented at all costs.'

German espionage had done a really thorough job. They were well informed about the defensive system as a whole

and particularly about its weak points. Apart from information provided by spies working in Holland, German Intelligence had on file a large number of up to date high-altitude photographs revealing troop concentrations and other defensive preparations in meticulous detail.

Speed and surprise, the Blitzkreig formula, were the vital factors. The plan centred on a quick take-over of the seat of government, The Hague,

and, if possible, the capture of the Queen. Troops were to be landed at three airfields near The Hague: Valkenburg, Ypenburg and Ockenburg, other air bases, and the Dutch air force, having been eliminated the previous night by bombing raids from the west. The strike force was to travel on motorcycles to The Hague at top speed and effect the capture of General Winkelman and other government ministers. They were also to take over the military offices, requisition cars (they even had a list of garages) and arrest everyone known to be, or suspected of, working for the Dutch, French or British Intelligence services. If the Queen were captured she would be required to issue the order to capitulate 'in order to avoid unnecessary bloodshed', though if she refused she was merely to be kept prisoner in her palace 'under honourable conditions'. Meanwhile the 9th Tank Division of the Eighteenth Army would be moving via Moerdijk and Dordrecht to Rotterdam, airborne troops from The Hague having secured the Moerdijk and Dordrecht bridges and occupied Waalhaven airfield near Rotterdam.

This, briefly, was the plan. How was Holland to defend herself with her small and ill equipped forces? General Reynders' request, in 1937, that sixty tanks be purchased was refused by the Minister of War, he being of the opinion that tanks were out of date; now Holland did not possess even one.

The Military Attaché at the Dutch Embassy in London was informed that Hitler's tanks were to pass through Brabant, on the reception of which news the decision was taken to order more than 140 tanks, but they had still not arrived by May 1940. The greater part of the Dutch army moved afoot, and communications were very primitive, despite the presence in Holland of the firm of Philips, one of Europe's most important companies making telecommunication machinery. Three-fifths of the troops were infantry, using old Austrian model rifles of

1890. There were very few hand grenades and many of the soldiers in any case had no training in their use.

One could go on indefinitely listing the shortcomings of the Dutch forces. They consisted in the main of conscripts with a too short and very primitive training, as there was no enthusiasm for the regular army and the number of regular officers had shrunk steadily. Among the reserve officers skilled military men were non-existent.

Since the Napoleonic wars and the separation of Belgium from the Netherlands, nothing dramatic had happened and this circumstance had promoted an indolence which dulled foresight. It was difficult to recognize that Holland might not be able to

Infantry of the Netherlands move to their defensive positions before the German assault. The cameraman can hardly have been aware of the painfully accurate symbolism in the figure whetting the stone

40

keep her neutrality.

One person who did realise the danger, and demonstrated her concern, was Queen Wilhelmina. She allowed for the possibility that she might have to leave her country and took thought for the safety of her daughter, Princess Juliana, and her family, who could find shelter in the neighbourhood of Paris with relatives of Prince Bernhard. Van Kleffens, Minister for Foreign Affairs, was the only one to know about the arrangements; he had digested the example of Warsaw as well and, fearing that The Hague might also be bombed, took steps to move the various ministries elsewhere.

Some others saw the writing on the wall: the Jews who emigrated; the companies who transferred their capital to Britain or the USA; the Netherlands Bank, which sent away the bulk of its gold reserves; Philips, who removed all their industrial patents and developments to Britain; and, significantly, the German Ambassador in The Hague, who deposited his vast personal fortune in the name of a friend in New York.

Finally, after the coldest winter for a century, came the spring. Hitler had been waiting with mounting impatience and now proposed 5th May for *Fall Gelb*. Minister van Kleffens, worried that it might be too late for the government to leave the country in case of an attack, sent a letter, dated 3rd May, to the Dutch Ambassador in London containing instructions to inform the heads of all Dutch overseas possessions that, should the Netherlands be forced to surrender, they were to continue to act independently as parts of the Dutch Kingdom. This was of particular importance for the Netherlands East Indies, as Japan had a more than normal interest in the area.

Left: Dutch sailors march past at a review. Even this maritime nation's navy was seriously under-equipped
Above: Princess Juliana and her husband Prince Bernhard. Queen Wilhelmina clear-sightedly made arrangements for the safety of her daughter and family well before the invasion

At Schiphol airport all the aircraft were fuelled and ready to take off. The motorways were intentionally littered with stationary cars at about sixty yard intervals, allowing normal traffic through but preventing the roads' use as landing strips for aircraft.

But *Fall Gelb* was postponed yet again. Major Sas then gave the last warning in an interminable series: Germany would attack on 8th May. Queen Wilhelmina and King Leopold of Belgium tried to intervene to save the peace. Hitler was adamant. On 7th May all leave was again cancelled.

When the expected German offensive failed to occur, the Dutch army's 200,000 combat and 50,000 depot troops relaxed, along with everybody else. But not, this time, for long: the attack was launched at precisely 0355, 10th May 1940.

Rude awakening

The remorseless advance into neutral Holland

Opening of the airborne assault

How unexpected the attack was can be illustrated by the events at Bergen airfield, where twenty-three fighters were waiting with warmed-up engines for the expected order to take off. There came the sound of aircraft overhead and it was assumed that they were German bombers on their way to England. However, over the North Sea they turned and, coming in from the west, proceeded to bomb the airfield. Bergen and its fighters were eradicated before the war had properly begun.

Overall, it was a well organised invasion. Hundreds of planes dropped thousands of parachutists, their white canopies showing up sharply against the clear blue sky. A sprinkling of white clouds – exploding anti-aircraft shells – appeared, but few casualties were caused among the low flying Junkers. A number of Dutch fighters engaged the invading aircraft but they were no match for the superior Messerschmitts, and the planes they escorted flew on unhindered.

Amazingly enough, one airfield survived intact. Apparently the Germans did not know of the existence of the Ruigenhoek base and while all the other airfields were being heavily bombed a Dutch fighter pilot landed at Ruigenhoek, his plane shredded by bullets, and found all personnel asleep. They were not even aware that war had broken out.

The main centre of activity during the invasion was the vicinity of The Hague, where half of the *Luftlandekorps* – airborne troops – were to land. Of the three airfields in the area, Ypenburg, Ockenburg and Valkenburg, the last was still being built and was not yet considered usable because of the soft condition of the ground. This did not prevent the landing of

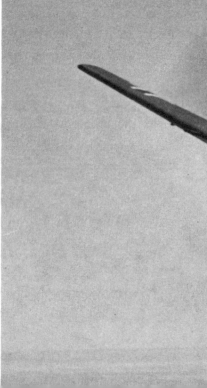

Escorted by Messerschmitt Bf 109s, better in every way than the planes of the Dutch air force, the bombers and transports initially suffered very few losses

Many of the German transports attempted forced landings. *Above:* a D617.
Below: a Ju 52

Above: A Dutch air force Fokker D-21. All these aircraft at Ypenburg field were out of action within an hour of the commencement of the air battle. *Below:* German paratroops soon after their drop. They put a halt to the gallant Dutch defence of Ypenburg

seventy-five German transports, however, though they were unable to take off again to make way for further landings. More than 1,000 German troops were landed here, twenty-one Dutch soldiers losing their lives in the operation.

Ypenburg was in use by the Dutch air force and was defended by a battalion of grenadiers. The waiting Fokker D-21s and Douglas fighters of the Dutch defence took off and managed to destroy five German planes, but within an hour all the D-21s were out of action because they had run out of fuel or ammunition or had themselves been destroyed. The Douglas aircraft fared even worse: eight were quickly shot down, one falling into a burning oil storage tank near Vlaardingen.

Some panic was caused among the Dutch soldiers by the bombing, one company commander reporting later that he had had to use brute force to control his unit – which for the most part consisted of cooks, batmen, clerks, etc having almost no weapons. This was the army upon which the defence of the Netherlands rested. However, when at 0524 the first German transports landed, the rest of the grenadiers fought well. All eight of the first wave of Junkers were riddled by bullets, some catching fire, and the following two eight-plane waves collided with those already on the ground with the obvious disastrous results. The fourth wave clearly could not hope to land successfully and were forced to turn away; some put down on the beach. The defenders had staved off the initial attack on Ypenburg, but before long the airfield fell to the advancing parachutists.

During the first few hours of the war the German air force had booked quite a success: most of the Dutch air force was destroyed, and that part of the Luftwaffe's mission could be considered to have gone roughly according to plan. But the attack on the governmental centre had fallen apart, for on not one of the three airfields around The Hague was it possible for German transport planes to land, and indeed at Ypenburg and Ockenburg the German troops were surrounded. Thus the lightning raid by motorcyclists on The Hague, aimed at capturing the Queen and Ministers, could not go forward.

The invasion forces had more success in the operations near Rotterdam, where Waalhaven airport, the bridges over the Meuse in Rotterdam and the large road bridges near Moerdijk and Dordrecht were occupied according to schedule.

Minister van Kleffens received a message that the German Ambassador in the Netherlands, Count Zech von Burkersroda, wished to see him at the Department. It proved difficult for the Minister to penetrate into The Hague; soldiers were blocking all entrances and every stranger was considered to be a member of the Fifth Column. Van Kleffens, though no stranger, had the greatest difficulty in persuading them to let him through, as they refused to believe that he was the Minister for Foreign Affairs – what would a Minister be doing in the middle of all that danger, where he would be quite likely to be shot by strafing German planes? A call to General Headquarters finally let him through. Count von Burkersroda had intended to read van Kleffens the transcript of the coded message received from his superiors, but when it came to the point he was so moved that he was unable to utter a word. He had been living in the Netherlands for twelve years and had made many friends during that time, and now his emotions were stirred to the extent that he was obliged to simply hand the piece of paper to van Kleffens. The substance of the message was that Germany had irrefutable proof that France and Britain intended to invade the Netherlands and Belgium with the aim of penetrating to the Ruhr Valley.

A rest by the roadside during the advance for the German troops

The Junkers Ju 87. During the Second World War the tactical dive-bomber was most successfully exemplified in the Junkers Ju 87. Although the type was often called the Stuka, this word is in fact a contraction of the German word *Sturzkampfflugzeug*, meaning 'dive bomber'; thus the term *Stuka* refers to all dive bombers and not to any particular one. Remarkably successful against unprepared enemy troops early in the war, when the Germans usually had air superiority, the Ju 87-equipped units suffered heavy losses when they were

The Heinkel He III. Numerically the most important bomber in the Luftwaffe during the first half of the war, the Heinkel He 111 saw service on all fronts. By the end of 1941 it was becoming out-dated, but because of development difficulties with the He 177 which should have replaced it, the older type continued in service until the end of the war. Also used as a transport and a glider tug. Specification of the He 111 H-6: *Engines:* Two Junkers Jumo 211s, each of which developed 1,340hp for take off. *Armament:* Up to 4,400 pounds of bombs, was the normal load, but in the overload condition a single 5,500-pound bomb could be carried; one 20mm cannon and five 7.9mm machine-guns. *Maximum speed:* 258mph at 16,400 feet. *Range:* 760 miles with maximum normal bomb load. *Ceiling:* 25,500 feet. *Weight:* Empty, 17,050 pounds; loaded, 27,400 pounds. *Span:* 74 feet 1½ inches. *Length:* 54 feet 5½ inches

ngaged by determined fighter pilots flying modern aircraft. Specification for
the Ju 87B-2: *Engine:* Junkers Jumo 211, developing 1,200hp for take off.
Armament: Either one 1,100-pound bomb or one 550 and four 110 pound bombs;
three 7.9mm machine-guns. *Maximum Speed:* 238mph at 13,400 feet. *Ceiling:*
26,200 feet. *Range:* 370 miles with a 1,100-pound bomb. *Weights:* Empty, 5,980
pounds; loaded, 9,560 pounds. *Span:* 45 feet 3½ inches. *Length:* 36 feet 5 inches.

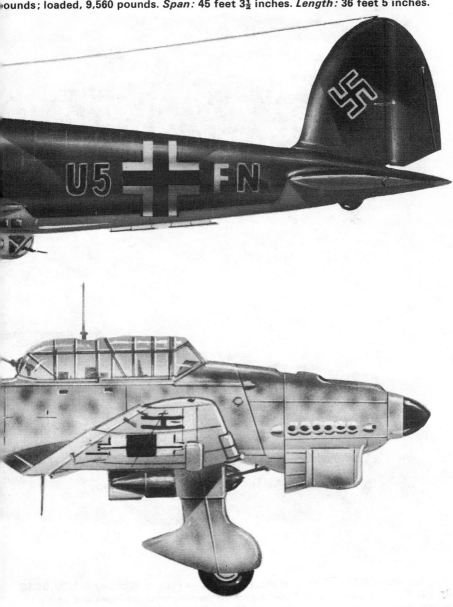

Me-109E-3 *Engine:* Daimler-Benz 601A, 1,100hp. *Armament:* 2 x 7.9mm machine-guns and 3 x 20mm cannon. *Speed:* 354mph at 12,300 ft. *Ceiling:* 37,500 feet, *Range:* 412 miles. *Weights:* 4,421-lbs empty and 5,523-lbs loaded. *Span:* 32 4½ ins. *Length:* 28 ft 3 ins.

The Douglas 8A-3N attack bomber. *Engine:* One Pratt & Whitney R-1830-SC3G radial, 1,050hp. *Armament:* Four .3-inch Browning machine-guns and up to 1,000-lbs of bombs. *Speed:* 255mph. *Climb:* 1,750 feet per minute initially. *Ceiling:* 29,800 feet. *Range:* 910 miles. *Weight:* empty/loaded: 5,370/8,948-lbs. *Span:* 47 feet 9 inches. *Length:* 32 feet 5 inches. *Crew:* 2

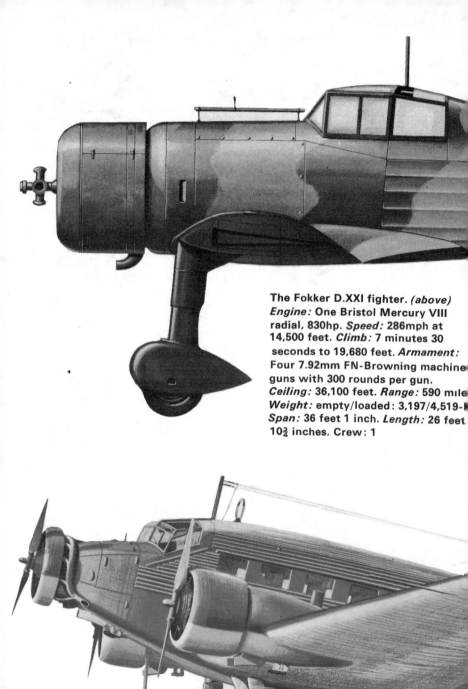

The Fokker D.XXI fighter. *(above)*
Engine: One Bristol Mercury VIII
radial, 830hp. *Speed:* 286mph at
14,500 feet. *Climb:* 7 minutes 30
seconds to 19,680 feet. *Armament:*
Four 7.92mm FN-Browning machine
guns with 300 rounds per gun.
Ceiling: 36,100 feet. *Range:* 590 mile
Weight: empty/loaded: 3,197/4,519-
Span: 36 feet 1 inch. *Length:* 26 feet
10¾ inches. Crew: 1

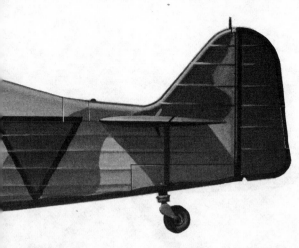

…e Junkers Ju 52. Originally designed as a single-engined transport, the Junkers 52 …st flew in its three-motored form in 1932. Before the war the type saw world-wide …rvice as an airliner, and it was ordered as a bomber/transport for the …-forming Luftwaffe. The Ju 52 did go into action as a bomber in Spain, but …sses were uncomfortably high and it was rapidly replaced in this role. The type …ent on to become the standard transport type in the Luftwaffe, and continued … service until the end of the war; other Ju 52s were used as trainers, others …ll were modified to explode magnetic mines from the air. Production …ntinued until 1944, and a total of 3,234 examples were built. **Specification for** …e Junkers Ju 52/3mg7e: *Engines:* Three BMW 132T motors developing 830hp for …ke off. *Armament:* One 13mm and two 7.9mm machine-guns. *Load:* 18 fully …uipped troops or an equivalent freight load. *Maximum speed:* 189mph. *Service* …*iling* 18,000 feet. *Normal Range* 930 miles. *Span:* 95 feet 10 inches. *Length:* 60 …et 8¼ inches.

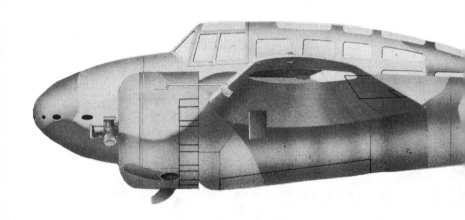

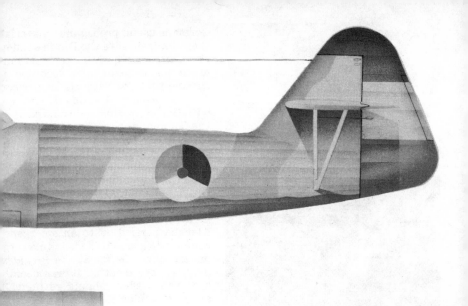

The Fokker T.VIII-W torpedo/reconnaissance floatplane. *Engines:* Two Wright Whirlwind R-975-E3 radials, 450hp each. *Armament:* Three 7.92mm FN-Browning machine-guns, and one torpedo or up to 1,300-lbs of bombs. *Speed:* 177mph. *Ceiling:* 22,300 feet. *Range:* 1,710 miles maximum. *Weight:* empty/loaded: 7,834/11,020-lbs. *Span:* 59 feet $\frac{2}{3}$ inch. *Length:* 42 feet 7$\frac{3}{4}$ inches. *Crew:* 3

The Fokker G.1a fighter. *Engines:* Two Bristol Mercury VIII radials, 830hp each. *Armament:* Eight fixed and one flexible FN-Browning 7.92mm machine-guns and up to 880-lbs of bombs. *Speed:* 295mph at 13,990 feet. *Climb:* 8 minutes 44 seconds to 19,680 feet. *Ceiling:* 30,500 feet. *Range:* 945 miles. *Weight:* empty/loaded: 7,326/10,560-lbs. *Span:* 56 feet 3$\frac{1}{4}$ inches. *Length:* 37 feet 8$\frac{3}{4}$ inches. *Crew:* 3.

Lord Halifax of the British Foreign Office, who held discussions with van Kleffens and Welter, Dutch Minister for the Colonies, on their arrival in London. Holland was now one of the Western Allies

Attempts at resistance to the German forces of occupation were useless since the enormous armies of Germany would crush them instantly. Dutch property and the Royal Family would, however, be guaranteed against abuse if the Dutch laid down their arms. If not, the country might expect total annihilation.

According to the Dutch Constitution war could not be declared without ratification by the *Staten-Generaal*, equivalent to both houses of the British Parliament. The war was, of course, in progress at that moment, so any declaration would in any case merely confirm the existing state of affairs. Van Kleffens, however, did not want to risk the possibility of critics being able to say that the Dutch had not declared war, as it would give the Germans useful propaganda material; they would declare the Dutch soldiers *Franc-tireurs*. The Minister therefore made his decision and recorded in writing that the Netherlands Government considered the country at war with Germany. He handed his reply to the Count and asked him if he had anything to say. Count Zech von Burkersroda could only stammer a few words of farewell, and as he left van Kleffens shook hands with him (offending two Dutch officers who were present). Von Burkersroda was removed for internment to the Hotel des Indes and van Kleffens hurried off to an emergency conference about to be held in a large underground shelter at the *Bezuidenhout*. At the meeting it was decided that van Kleffens should go immediately to London to describe the situation and ask for help. There was hardly any wind, something very rare in the Netherlands, and he proposed that in these ideal conditions a seaplane could take off from Scheveningen and carry him to the other side of the North Sea. Welter, Minister for the Colonies, was to accompany him, and van Kleffens requested that his wife be allowed to travel with him if there was room for her in the plane; this was agreed to.

At Scheveningen they found two seaplanes gently rocking in the calm sea, but one had its petrol tank shot to pieces and the other was listing badly because one of the floats was riddled with bullets. The pilot of the latter declared that if he could get up enough speed the water would be sucked out of the float and that they might be able to take off. They were lucky and got away under a rain of bullets. (Three days later the officer who had accompanied them to the beach arrived in London and told them that the other seaplane had been bombed immediately after they took off, killing three young sailors.)

In the excitement of the moment nobody had thought to check that there was a map in the aircraft, so the flight was accomplished by rule of thumb. After some time they saw a large coastal town to starboard and decided to come down – the town turned out to be Brighton. Listing dangerously they taxied to the waterfront, with 'Sparks' sitting on the wing waving his handkerchief. A crowd rapidly gathered on the beach, among them a great many policemen who escorted them to police headquarters in Brighton where they were given sandwiches – very welcome, for they had had nothing to eat since the night before. As they did not have any British currency, the police also bought them their train tickets to London. They were accompanied on the journey by the Mayor of Brighton, and on reaching the capital found the Dutch Ambassador waiting for them at the station. Wasting no time they went straight to the Foreign Office and there had a lengthy discussion with Lord Halifax; the Netherlands, having been attacked by Germany, was promoted from her neutral status to an ally. After the session with Lord Halifax they met the First Lord of the Admiralty, Winston Churchill, who had just received the news from Buckingham Palace that Chamberlain had resigned and that he was charged with forming a new cabinet. 'All were most kind', writes van Kleffens in *The Rape of The Netherlands*.

Now that two of its members were in London, the German invaders were not able to silence the voice of the legal government of the Netherlands, a fact which turned out to be of enormous importance, and the British Broadcasting Corporation offered van Kleffens the opportunity of speaking to the British people to tell them that he was there to build strong bonds with the governments of the powers of which they now had become an ally.

There were at this time four leading Dutch Shipowners in London; they decided to form a Shipping Committee that would be recognized by both the British and the Dutch Governments. The committee was to assume control of those ships of the Dutch Merchant Fleet which had been, or might be, able to escape the Germans. At that moment there were about forty-five Dutch ships in the harbours of Britain.

Welter and van Kleffens were received in audience by the King the day after their arrival and were most impressed by his personality and the sympathy and kindness he showed them.

Meanwhile the Dutch Royal Family was in the Huis ten Bosch Palace, just outside The Hague, where there was a large underground shelter. Early in the morning a German plane flew low over the palace and, though it was shot down, the incident made Queen Wilhelmina realize that it was time to take more positive steps for the safety of the Crown Princess and her two

Queen Wilhelmina, Princess Juliana and Princess Armgard (mother of Prince Bernhard) with Crown Princess Beatrix. The Queen decided that it was high time to leave the area of the Hague with the Royal Family when an enemy plane flew low over the Huis ten Bosch Palace

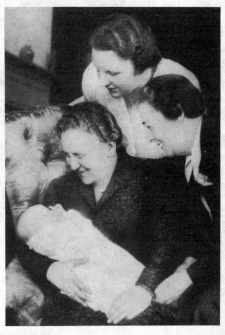

small daughters, and she decided that they should leave the country immediately. But the three airfields near The Hague were littered with stranded German transport planes and were unusable, and fighting in the vicinity of Waalhaven airfield precluded its use. And the woods around Huis ten Bosch were teeming with German airborne troops. General Winkelman advised the Royal Family to move for the time being to the Palace of Noordeinde in The Hague, where they would be a little safer. To be as unobtrusive as possible the Court automobiles were left behind and two ordinary vehicles were used, Queen Wilhelmina travelling in the leading car, the Crown Princess and her family following. Because of the many rumours of the existence of a Fifth Column (there was talk of unknown and mysterious persons sniping at Dutch soldiers) they were surprised to find their journey as uneventful as it proved. They were able to reach the Noordeinde Palace quite easily, and from there it was arranged, via a radio connection with the British Admiralty, that Princess Juliana and her daughters would embark late at night on ships of the squadron that the British were dispatching to IJmuiden, originally to ship out the gold of the Netherlands Bank. However, the country between The Hague and IJmuiden was now extremely unsafe because of the presence of German airborne troops, and the departure was postponed.

In Rotterdam the battle was in full blast, and by early morning the Germans had taken the bridges over the Maas in the centre of Rotterdam; Waalhaven airfield had also been captured and in the course of the day almost 6,000 German soldiers were landed there. The Dutch, in fact, had about 7,000 troops guarding the depots and harbour installations, but of these only 1,000 were adequately trained and even they had the use of only eight heavy and forty-eight light and antiquated machine-guns. They were taken completely by surprise, moreover, not having been alerted during the night of 9th-10th May, and had no good idea of what exactly was going on. Germany had been expected to attack the Netherlands over the common frontier, not from the other side of the country via the harbour city of Rotterdam in the West. They were also the victims of all kinds of rumours – for instance that the Germans were disguised as Dutch policemen and that members of the Fifth Column were shooting on Dutch soldiers. In short, it was an enormously chaotic situation, much to the advantage of the German Commander-in-Chief, General Student.

The defensive measures the Dutch were able to put in hand were pitifully inadequate compared with the powers trying to take the city. Colonel Scharroo, the Commander of Rotterdam, had seen to it that all the entrances to the city were barricaded; the *Z5*, an old torpedo boat lying near the Hook-of-Holland, sailed to the Willemsbrug, together with the *TM 51*, the only torpedo boats which the Dutch Navy had in the Netherlands, to attack the Germans. They were bombed persistently by German aircraft, and though luckily all the bombs missed their targets, firing from the shore caused them enough trouble. It was arranged that they would be reinforced by the destroyer *Van Galen*, just back home from the Dutch East Indies, and two gun boats from Den Helder, but before the *Van Galen* could reach Rotterdam German dive bombers sent her to the bottom after she had shot down three of them.

But help was on the way. The French Seventh Army, stationed at the Franco-Belgian border, had been ordered to move up to the north immediately. However, this was not a simple matter, as transport for such a force was not readily available. It was accomplished by rail and a diversity

German infantry load a light artillery piece and assorted weaponry aboard a rubber dinghy on the Maas

Here and overleaf: more men
and supplies cross the Maas

The invading troops survey the opposite bank at Maastricht

of requisitioned automobiles, quite rickety according to an eye witness who saw them pass by in Belgium: 'discarded Paris omnibuses, moving vans, transport lorries once used to bring vegetables to *Les Halles* in Paris and the delivery vans of big department stores'. The French artillery was drawn by small aggressive horses. Those unlucky troops without transport had to travel on foot. The French Commander-in-Chief, General Gamelin, realizing all too well how time consuming this business would be, ordered an advance force to be sent to Flushing in Zeeland by means of a cargo vessel under a guard of warships. In the course of the day the first consignment arrived, the scouting group under the command of Colonel de Beauchesne. In addition the British troops landed.

Early in the morning of 10th May

London had instructed demolition parties to be ready for action, one detachment to go to IJmuiden to destroy the floodgates while they were open. Fortunately the commander at IJmuiden was able to prevent this happening; if the plan had gone through the whole West of the Netherlands would have been inundated by the sea – a total disaster.

The detachment sent to Rotterdam had the job of setting fire to the oil tanks of Pernis, just outside Rotterdam. General Winkelman, however, had already ordered preparations to be made to render the oils useless; simply mixing the various kinds of oils would achieve the same result as destroying them by fire – in the short term. He considered premature such drastic measures as igniting and blowing up oil-installations. During the night of 10th-11th May the British detachment helped with the loading aboard ship of twenty-two million guilders' worth of gold bars from the

Netherlands Bank. There was still more gold to come, but by daylight a halt was called as the bank building was being fired on. The British vessel was sunk by a magnetic mine soon after she left and the commander lost his life. During the occupation the Germans were able to recover four-fifths of the gold lying on the bottom of the *Nieuwe Waterweg;* they called it spoils of war and transported it to Germany. But the rest of the gold still in Amsterdam was brought over to England safely in two cargo ships of the KNSM escorted by British cruisers. Gold to the value of more than 887 million Dutch guilders was saved from the greed of the Third Reich.

Two old ferryboats of the Harwich Line – the *Malines* and the *St Denis* – were moored in Rotterdam ready to take off the staff of the British Consulate (and also persons working for the British Secret Service) in case of a German attack. Vrinten and his close collaborator Koutrik (now a double agent working for the *Abwehr*) were among those who fled to Britain on one of these, the *Malines.* Unfortunately Koutrik knew of the whereabouts of Vrinten's dossiers and other records, which information he did not fail to pass to the Germans. Many 'contacts' were arrested, and some even executed.

Germany, in the meantime, ruled the air over Holland. The Dutch pilots fought back with selfless courage and determination but were at a serious disadvantage in their old and slow machines, and the first day of the war saw the destruction of twenty per cent of their inadequate aircraft. The anti-aircraft gunners, lacking experience in shooting at moving targets, gained that experience rapidly during the first hours of the morning of 10th May; they managed to shoot down about a hundred transport planes, but in that brief period alone half the total stock of anti-aircraft ammunition was used up. Including aircraft which could no longer take off, as described earlier, 200 German transport planes were

General Gamelin, French C-in-C, had the task of moving his Seventh Army to the scene of the conflict with little in the way of transport

lost.

Despite the disastrous fact that the Germans were in possession of the bridges over the Maas in Rotterdam and the bridges near Dordrecht and Moerdijk, hope was still strong at the Dutch military headquarters that it would be possible to find a way to connect up with the French troops then marching up, and halt the German assault.

The German generals who were besieging Rotterdam were, in fact, very pessimistic. They recognized that the air attacks near The Hague had for the most part failed. Only thirteen of the first fifty-five transport aircraft had returned to base, and one of these still had its entire load on board. A worried General Kesselring sent a scout plane to The Hague which returned with the message that nothing special could be observed. He con-

The Dutch anti-aircraft units quickly remedied their lack of experience during the first hours of the invasion but used half their ammunition stocks in the process

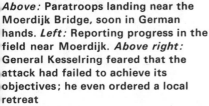

Above: Paratroops landing near the Moerdijk Bridge, soon in German hands. *Left:* Reporting progress in the field near Moerdijk. *Above right:* General Kesselring feared that the attack had failed to achieve its objectives; he even ordered a local retreat

cluded that the attack had failed and decided to retreat in the direction of Delft (half-way between The Hague and Rotterdam). He attempted to send an order to that effect to the group encamped near Valkenburg but could get no connection.

General Student had told the German commander who had taken the *Noordereiland* that it was quite possible that it would take another two weeks before the 9th Panzer-Division could come to their aid. But General von Bock, the commander of *Heeresgruppe* B of the 9th Panzer-Division, was determined to push through. He knew that a great deal had gone wrong in the west of the Netherlands,

but the Moerdijk bridge was taken and that was, as he wrote in his diary, the main thing. The most important goals, the bridges near Gennep, Moerdijk, Dordrecht and Rotterdam, were achieved, and the Germans would not let go.

Among the Dutch panic was rife, and not merely the civilian population was affected; morale had collapsed in the military sector also, and there were a great many unsubstantiated rumours abroad – for instance that the Germans were about to use gas. But there was especially a fear of a Fifth Column (a term originating in the Spanish Civil War) which caused much exaggerated and counter-helpful suspicion. Priests and monks, for some reason, above all were suspect, and after the story got around that German airborne troops had landed dressed in blue smocks, brown trousers and wooden shoes, every farmer had to undergo the most searching scrutiny.

Every German residing in the Netherlands was arrested, including a great many Jews; there was not enough room to house all the prisoners adequately and appalling overcrowding resulted. Hundreds of people were imprisoned in the big hall of the KLM building. Some of the Jews were heard to remark that they would be better off in the German concentration camps, for there there was at least the opportunity to wash oneself.

In the meantime the French had arrived in the south of the country. Together with a Dutch detachment they attempted to recapture the Moerdijk bridge, but the Luftwaffe bombed and machine-gunned the force incessantly and the attack failed. Communication lapses and other difficulties gave rise to confusion in which again rumour took the place of facts. The French, not having been informed

German tanks in Holland. The French Commander Lestoquoi was captured when he inadvertently came face to face with the armour of 9th Panzer Division

of the order that troops in the south were to retreat behind the big rivers in *Vesting Holland* considered that they, the French, were being deserted by the Dutch Army.

Colonel Schmidt, commanding the 'Peel-Division' in the South Netherlands, who was charged with the defence of the province Noord-Brabant, did not have an easy task. During the morning of the 11th May he had lost contact with most of his battalion commanders, one of whom, reserve-major Döbken, had already been killed by a German machine-gun he was trying to destroy. Other commanders had changed their positions without leaving any message as to where they could be reached. The situation was further worsened by the French making contradictory demands; Lieutenant-Colonel Lestoquoi wished to post his troops south of Breda, other French commanders north of Breda. Unfortunately the colonel was not aware of the fact that there were

Dutch military transport strafed by the Luftwaffe

several hundred members of the Royal Constabulary in Breda whom he could have used for directing the disorganised troops. Telephone messages tended to be intentionally obscure, because everybody feared that Fifth Columnists were listening in.

Lestoquoi decided to go in person to Roosendaal, where his staff had moved, for information he needed. He chose a road parallel to the main highway – and bumped into the first tanks of 9th Panzer Division. He was taken prisoner and brought to Den Bosch (Bois-le-Duc), where he was subjected to a thorough interrogation. Questioned about the whereabouts of the Light Division of III Army Corps he was quite unable to answer, even supposing he had wished, because he had not a clue himself. Thus the Commander of the Peel Division was eliminated, but by now that made no difference; the roads swarmed with fleeing soldiers, without their field

kitchens or provisions, without medical assistance, unorganised, walking, bicycling, or in requisitioned cars, unceasingly strafed and bombed by German aircraft. A particularly bad stretch was the road between Tilburg and Breda which, though strewn with the bodies of soldiers and horses and with burning vehicles and therefore virtually impassable, continued to receive the attention of the German fighters.

General Student, who had captured the island of IJsselmonde in the south where Waalhaven airfield was, just outside Rotterdam, was reinforced by another 750 men delivered by air, and also replenishment of his stocks of material. The Dutch soldiers of the Light Division tried all possible ways of reaching the island, but were always driven back, and the story was repeated near the Oude Maas, where the

More paratroops swell the ranks of
Kurt Student's force on IJsselmonde

A Dutch 10cm gun is stripped for action. Shortage of ammunition and counter-bombardment hampered the Dutch gunners

The fire-gutted hulk of the Holland-Amerika liner *Statendam.* Used as a machine-gun platform by the Germans she was shelled by the Dutch, starting the conflagration which ate its way through the whole interior of the ship

Germans had also dug themselves in solidly. The lack of training of the Dutch military leaders was a factor which everywhere hindered the defence; it crippled, for instance, the attack on the bridge near Barendrecht, and the same was the case in Rotterdam itself. The troops stationed there, as nearly everywhere in Holland, had had little or no training; some were raw young recruits who had not even been given the chance to learn how to use a gun.

General Winkelman withdrew three battalions of the reserves near the Grebbeberg to help Rotterdam; together with a fourth battalion which had been first sent to Leyden, they formed a much needed reinforcement for the extremely nervous and quite inadequate army force which had the task of defending the city. They totalled many more than the probably only 1,000 Germans who had captured Rotterdam-South, the bordering Noorder Islands and the small bridgehead at the north end of the Willemsbrug. There was an attempt to drive the German troops out of their dominating positions by means of bombardments (necessarily light) but

to no avail. Because of interdicting fire from the Noorder Island it was not possible to place the artillery in position; the only artillery to be in the required position on the north shore of the river on the 10th of May had been brought over to Hillegersberg, where it was judged that it would be of more use. In addition, the observation post on the Maas tunnel ventilators could not be used, and consequently the artillery, which had been firing regularly at Waalhaven, could not direct its fire for some time. Disabled German planes on the airfield had more than four undisturbed hours in which to be repaired; the bombardment was not resumed until long after they had departed.

By far the majority of the Dutch troops were being used purely defensively. There was such apprehension that the Germans would cross the Maas at other points that enormous effort was put into building up the defence front, quite unnecessarily, in tremendous haste. And even this misdirected aim was hamstrung by the confusion reigning among the officers directing operations and the suspicion that the Fifth Column was operating. At this time Dutch soldiers not infrequently fired on their comrades, imagining them to be either Germans in disguise or renegade Dutch.

In the morning the Commander of the British destroyer *Wild Swan* offered to sail up the Nieuwe Maas to

Rotterdam and shell Waalhaven with his ship's guns. This offer was not accepted because of the risk to Dutch troops who had been ordered to re-capture Waalhaven. At 1230 the same commander was instructed by the Admiralty to execute the operation anyhow, but the bombardment still did not take place because of rumours in the Hook of Holland that Waalhaven had been recaptured. Thus the Dutch at the Maas had to make do with virtually no artillery support. En-gagements were taking place every-where at this juncture and the Witte Huis, or White House, a local land-mark of importance because of its strategic position, had to be aban-doned.

A fire which had started at the Boompjes was now spreading and a number of ships in the Wijnhaven were ablaze. A choking, stinking smoke hung over the nearby parts of Rotter-dam. During the afternoon the Ger-mans set up machine-guns on the *Statendam* of the Holland-Amerika Line, moored in the Wijnhaven. The crew succeeded in escaping despite being ordered to remain below decks, and the Dutch commenced firing at the beautiful ship causing, naturally, considerable damage and starting fires – and causing also great indignation among the board of directors of the Holland-Amerika Line, who asked the military authorities why the ship could not be sunk with a single well-

The *Dinteldijk* and many other large vessels berthed at Rotterdam during the invasion also burned out

aimed shot. This, apparently, was not possible. A fire float which went to the *Statendam* to try to extinguish the fires, turned back when its commander was killed. In the evening the ship, not yet eleven years old, was one enormous fireball. The same fate overtook the vessels *Dinteldijk*, *Bosdijk* and *Veendam*.

The civilian population of the Noorder Island suffered badly; on the 10th May the gas and water supply systems ceased to function, and on the 11th, when all the buildings at the west end of the island were burning like flares, the quays had to be evacu-ated. Thousands were forced to shelter in schools and other large buildings; in the Catholic school alone there were 500 people, many of whom had their pets with them. There were only two WCs in the school and, of course, they were without water. A German who had been living in the Netherlands for many years and who was an ardent opponent of the Nazi regime, volun-teered for a dangerous mission. His business had been destroyed the day before, he had ulcers, he was a Jew, and he had no living relatives; he valued his life no more for its own sake and wanted to be of some use to his fellow men. There was a pressing need for water for all purposes, and he repeatedly fetched water from the

A taste of what was to come; buildings begin to burn

Prins Hendrikkade, risking his life every time he went.

Those who still possessed an intact house seldom went outside. But German troops had started to enter houses to order men and boys to dig trenches. Choltitz was determined to try to keep the Noorder Island and the Willemsbrug to the very end, hoping for the arrival in time of 9th Panzer Division. He ignored General Student's order to abandon the small bridgehead on the north shore on the evening of 11th May.

With the only two bombers which the Dutch Air Force still possessed an attempt was made to destroy the Willemsbrug and eliminate the German bridgehead on Noorder Island.

The bombs missed the bridge but many fell on houses on the west end of Noorder Island and caused fires which made thousands more people homeless. In the afternoon the attempt was repeated, but again to no avail. On their return the tiny bombing force encountered twelve German fighters and lost a bomber and a fighter leaving the Dutch Air Force with only one bomber.

The second day of the war had been a catastrophe. East of the Grebbe Line the strip of outposts had been lost; the Peel-Raam position had been abandoned; the defence of the Zuid Willemsvaart had crumbled and the Dutch troops in Noord-Brabant were panic-stricken. The Light Division had not succeeded in crossing the Noord and ousting the German troops from IJsselmond Island; the 6th Border

Dietrich von Choltitz. The General was determined to retain Noorder Island and the Willemsbrug until the arrival of 9th Panzer Division

Battalion had failed at the bridgehead at Moerdijk and the 3rd was marooned near Barendrecht at the Oude Maas. In Rotterdam the Germans expanded their small foothold at the north end of the Willemsbrug, and all attacks on their airborne troops near Delft, The Hague, Wassenaar and Valkenburg had been repulsed.

Half the ammunition for the Dutch anti-aircraft guns was used up on the first day of war. The modern heavy batteries had been supplied by Vickers of England, from whence further supplies of ammunition would have to come. But an urgent request by the Dutch military attaché in London to give priority to the Dutch order met with the reply that there was none of the calibre required in stock.

The invaders were certain that it would not be difficult to break Dutch resistance. From their air reconnaissance they knew that the Dutch were short of artillery for the defence of the Grebbeberg outpost strip, but whether or not the Dutch defended the Grebbeberg to the last man was considered of minor importance, since 9th Panzer Division was expected to penetrate very shortly to Rotterdam via Moerdijk and Dordrecht. This meant that far behind the Dutch troops who were defending the Grebbe Line and the New Water Line, 150 heavy German tanks could make directly for The Hague, for the seat of the Dutch government and the residence of the Royal Family.

The German infantry who stormed the
Peel-Raam position march on to new
conquests

Days
three and four

12th May, Whit Sunday, tanks of h Panzer Division reached the oerdijk bridge. The 'Won' position the north of the Netherlands, eant for the defence of the Afsluit-jk, was taken and there was heavy ;hting near the Grebbe Line (in the st of Holland). In the neighbourhood Wageningen the Germans began a avy artillery bombardment which ie Dutch were unable to halt.

In Rotterdam-Zuid and elsewhere i IJsselmonde Island General Student ad been fortunate in finding about a indred trucks which he used to ansport a full battalion of airborne oops, three artillery batteries and me anti-aircraft guns. By approxi-mately one o'clock that afternoon the column had passed over the Oude Maas and not long afterwards they attacked and took the railway station of Dordrecht and the area surround-ing. A gas-holder caught fire and illuminated the neighbourhood when dusk set in.

Towards 1700, scouts of 9th Panzer Division, light armoured cars, started to pass over the Moerdijk bridge. A Dutch ensign, prisoner since the morning, and who himself saw the armoured cars approaching on the highway in the centre of the island of Dordrecht, was ordered to go to the commanding officer of the Dutch troops on the island and to recommend him to surrender. The commander in question was Colonel van der Bijl, in charge of the Light Division which had just succeeded in crossing to the island, and who had settled his post in Dubbeldam, about one mile from Dordrecht. He immediately took up the telephone to inform the com-mander of Fortress Holland, General van Andel. The general assumed that van der Bijl had merely heard rumours about approaching armoured vehicles, and he had learned from General Winkelman that there were French armoured cars on their way to support them, so it could only be the French. German armoured cars? Impossible . . . and van der Bijl himself had not had time to verify independently the message the ensign had brought. The colonel in the meantime was on his way to Dordrecht, to deal with changes in the command of the artillery. (His mission involved one Lieutenant-Colonel Mussert, brother of Mussert the NSB leader, who was under a well-founded suspicion of unreliability, and of whom we shall hear more later. Van der Bijl deprived Mussert of the command of the Dordrecht artillery but General van Andel reversed the dismissal though placing Mussert under van der Bijl's direct command.)

An anti-aircraft post on a demolished rail bridge

Above left: German artillery moves up to intensify the bombardment. *Above:* General Kurt Student. About a hundred trucks were commandeered on the general's orders and used to transport troops and artillery for the attack on Dordrecht. *Left:* Dutch POWs pleased – at least in this German photograph – to be prisoners

Anti-tank gun of the Dutch army in action against 9th Panzer Division

The Colonel's journey was not a simple matter. The German force had already penetrated between Dubbeldam and Dordrecht. He decided to make a detour with his combat staff and reach Dordrecht via the railroad west of Sliedrecht, where he would be able to cross to Dordrecht by means of the Papendrecht ferry boat. Late at night he arrived at Papendrecht only to find the ferry boat moored at the other side of the river and out of order.

Now the commander of the Light Division was cut off from the island of Dordrecht and from all the troops stationed there. And not only were the scout cars of 9th Panzer Division there, the first heavy tanks had also arrived. During the night the Dutch troops retreated to the Dordrecht town centre, extremely tired, famished and demoralised. Not one of their attacks had succeeded, and one Ger-

The tanks race for Rotterdam

man aircraft after another had come over without the appearance of a single Allied plane.

The Dutch troops positioned opposite Willemsdorp on Beijerland, on the west shore of the Kil, had seen armoured cars crossing the Moerdijk bridge in the afternoon, but it had not been possible to determine whether they were German or French. Nevertheless they fired on the vehicles and were proved correct in their decision when they were bombed and machine-gunned by twenty German bombers in the early evening of 12th May. They continued to harry the bridge traffic until the afternoon of the following day. The German commander in Willemsdorp assumed that he could expect a landing in force on the island, in which a full Dutch regiment would take part, reinforced by British troops.

The Dutch batteries near the Moer-

Loading a round into the breech of a gun of a Dutch coastal battery

dijk bridges were desperately in need of ammunition. Twelve tons of ammunition, destined for the batteries in Beijerland, had arrived in trucks on Saturday and was loaded aboard the motor-vessel *De Twee Gezusters* (the Two Sisters). She attempted to sail under the German-held bridge but heavy gunfire forced her to turn back to Gorinchem – with twelve tons of explosives aboard the ship was little more than a floating bomb. A further attempt was made with a crew of service volunteers and, escorted by the gunboat *Christiaan Cornelis*, they sailed towards Dordrecht. Incredibly, they were not fired on at the Moerdijk bridges, but on the Dordtse Kil they were subjected to shelling from the island and strafing by aircraft. The *Christiaan Cornelis* was forced to turn back, heavily damaged, to the Hollands Diep, towed by the tug *Robur*,

which had also suffered considerably but the *Twee Gezusters*, still under attack, succeeded in reaching the little harbour of Strijensas, outside Dordrecht, where the ammunition was unloaded with the utmost speed. Her captain was dead and the steersman severely wounded.

During the night panic had broken out in the anti-aircraft HQ at Dordrecht and the telephone installation there had been demolished. This unnecessary destruction was caused by another instance of rumour being accepted as fact. A message had come through that the enemy was marching along the Coolsingel and, so that nothing of any value would be left for the Germans to use, the equipment was smashed and the staff fled. The Post Office maintenance department reinstalled the main lines on 12th May, but communications suffered greatly in the interim.

In Rotterdam the garrison commander, Colonel Scharroo, had re-eived reinforcements of five battalions on 10th and 11th May, and in view of this it seemed inexplicable that the Germans were still in possession of the Maas bridges. General Winkelman ordered Lieutenant-Colonel Wilson to Rotterdam, together with two other staff officers, Wilson having been given full authority to replace Scharroo if that should seem necessary. When Wilson, accompanied by three armoured cars, arrived in Rotterdam, he found that the troops were being fully used to protect the town on the west, north and east and for manning the extended Maas boundary. Moreover, many detachments were searching houses for fifth columnists.

The first two German bombings, in the morning of Whit Sunday, had destroyed the eye hospital and a number of houses between Oostplein and Beurs Station. For security reasons Scharroo moved his headquarters to the Blijdorp district in the north of the city.

Wilson came to the conclusion that it was not feasible to use the troops at present in Rotterdam for an attack over the Maas bridges. He telephoned for further reinforcements and was promised that the 2nd Battalion of the *Jagers* (Hunters) Regiment, located in the Hook of Holland, would be sent to Rotterdam. At 1400 the commander of 2nd Battalion received the order to march immediately with his unit to Rotterdam. One of his companies, however, was spread over Rozenburg Island. Not until 0130 the following day was the battalion ready to leave for Rotterdam, almost twelve hours after the order had been received, time which the Germans used to dig themselves in near the Maas bridges. Wilson, who had taken the road via Gouda to Rotterdam because he assumed that the road through Delft was occupied by the Germans, wished to check his assumption and sent one of the three armoured cars to Delft. There was some shooting near Overschie but apart from that the armoured car reached Delft unhindered. The road was lined with wrecked and abandoned German vehicles.

The 1st Division Commander's order to attack in the direction of Rotterdam via Delft was not changed. Parachutists were seen descending near Rotterdam. The attackers got to within about one-and-a-half miles of Overschie, firing meanwhile at the parachutists, but did not succeed in reaching the town. The remnant of the 22nd Luftlande Division which had been ordered to retreat south of Delft had gone further south and had arrived in Overschie on 12th May. From them had come the shots aimed at Wilson's armoured car. More troops moved to Overschie, where there were no Dutch troops to offer resistance, on the same day.

There was not much left of the Dutch air force. Some few fighters and the only remaining bomber tried to attack near the Won position but they could not break through the defence put up by the German aircraft. Success would not have made much difference for the Won position was at that time already in German hands.

They were only slightly more successful near Wageningen. To raise the morale of the Dutch ground-staff General van Voorst tot Voorst had asked for air force aid to attack targets west of Wageningen. One of the pilots of the slow and very old-fashioned C-5s told later how he could see Wageningen far away wrapped in a blanket of smoke and flames. He aimed in that direction and was suddenly pounced on by three German fighters – Messerschmitt 109s or Heinkel 112s – much faster and heavily armed. He dived away in a hail of bullets and tracer, and then discovered that the machine refused to answer to the controls, and before he had a chance to bail out the aircraft hit a dyke under full power and somersaulted to the ground. When the pilot regained consciousness he found himself drenched with petrol, the plane upside down and the leaking fuel tank distributing its

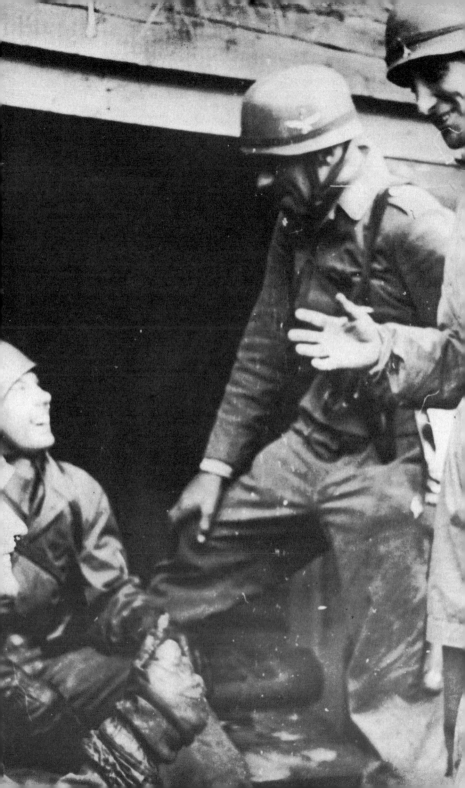

German parachutists, *Above:* looking for targets in the Rotterdam area, and, *Left:* relaxing in a quiet period

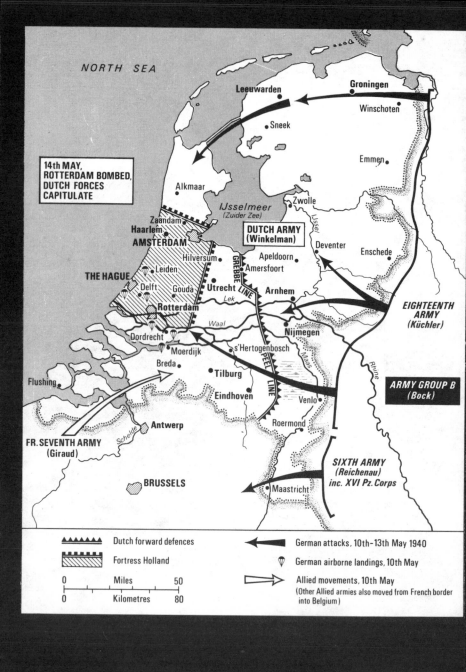

NORTH SEA

Groningen
Leeuwarden
Winschoten
Sneek
Emmen

**14th MAY,
ROTTERDAM BOMBED,
DUTCH FORCES
CAPITULATE**

Alkmaar
Zwolle
IJsselmeer
(Zuider Zee)
Zaandam
**DUTCH ARMY
(Winkelman)**
Haarlem
Deventer
Enschede
AMSTERDAM
Hilversum
Apeldoorn
Amersfoort
THE HAGUE
Leiden
Arnhem
**EIGHTEENTH
ARMY
(Küchler)**
Delft
Gouda
Utrecht
Lek
Rotterdam
Waal
Nijmegen
Dordrecht
Moerdijk
s'Hertogenbosch
**ARMY GROUP B
(Bock)**
Breda
Maas
Flushing
Tilburg
Venlo
Eindhoven
FR. SEVENTH ARMY
(Giraud)
Roermond
Antwerp
Schelde
**SIXTH ARMY
(Reichenau)
inc. XVI Pz. Corps**
BRUSSELS
Maastricht

GREBBE LINE
PEEL LINE
IJssel
Rhine

▲▲▲▲▲▲	Dutch forward defences	◄■■■	German attacks, 10th-13th May 1940
▓▓▓▓	Fortress Holland	♟	German airborne landings, 10th May
0	Miles 50	▷	Allied movements, 10th May
0	Kilometres 80		(Other Allied armies also moved from French border into Belgium)

ontents over the hot exhaust pipes. None of the bombs, which were still attached to the plane, had exploded in the collision. The pilot's foot was stuck but eventually he managed to free himself and get clear of the wreckage.

All in all, forty-eight missions were completed on 12th May, but little was gained.

The early surrender of the Won position had been a deep disappointment for General Winkelman, and he was very pessimistic about the whole situation: the bridges near Moerdijk, Dordrecht and in Rotterdam were still in German hands and the outposts strip near the Grebbe Line had not been recaptured either. The Luftwaffe was overwhelmingly strong and Dutch ammunition stocks were coming to an end (less than a quarter of the anti-aircraft ammunition was left). He told the Cabinet that the war would be lost in a few days at the most unless help came from the Allies very soon, and the Netherlands would have to capitulate. An urgent telegram sent to the British Government stated that the situation was so bad that without Allied help it was impossible to bring the German advance to a halt, and resistance would soon have to cease. Only immediate aid could save the issue. Dijxhoorn also called van Kleffens in London. He was lucky, for van Kleffens had an appointment with Churchill who had been, since 10th May, Prime Minister and Minister of Defence, but Churchill regretted not being able to be of help in the way requested. Van Kleffens had asked for three divisions, but the only troops available belonged to the Territorial Army, a kind of Civil Guard. The Royal Navy, however, was another matter. Churchill undertook to order all available destroyers to the Waddenzee (the waters between the islands and the north coast of the Netherlands) and shell the Afsluitdijk from there, which did not sound a bad idea at all. In the event, however, three motor torpedo boats sailed through

the Noordzeekanaal to the IJselmeer and on the Waddenzee itself only one destroyer appeared, for a very short time, on 13th May. The Royal Air Force bombed Waalhaven airfield, but not with much success. All in all, a purely token gesture.

The Germans had encountered stronger resistance at the Grebbe Line than they had anticipated, but they were not over-concerned since 9th Panzer Division had reached the Moerdijk bridge from the south. Hitler made the most of his success by adding to the 9th Panzer Division the 22nd Luftwaffe Division which, together with 7th Flieger Division and the SS Leibstandarte 'Adolf Hitler' – moved from the Veluwe (Gelderland) to Noord-Brabant, formed XXXIX Armee-Korps, under the command of *Generalleutnant der Panzertruppen* R Schmidt.

General Winkelman did not discover that the German tanks had reached the island of Dordrecht until he learned of it at 2330 via Radio Bremen. The situation was therefore even worse than he had assumed earlier and he prepared for an interview in the small hours with the Queen and Cabinet, to inform them of the gravity of the situation. When he arrived at half past three in the morning he did not have to wait long to pay his respects to the Queen. She had been occupied by the matter of shelter and security for her daughter and her family, and she had not been able to sleep since the truck supplied by the Netherlands Bank took them, late at night, to the British vessel waiting for them. When she heard from Winkelman that the outlook was extremely serious and that only massive Allied help could hope to solve their difficulties, she decided to telephone the King of England. The general agreed that such personal contact might achieve results, and at 0415 King George VI was woken by a police sergeant who told him that the Queen of the Netherlands was on the phone. 'I did not believe him', the King wrote in his diary, 'but I went to the phone and it was her. She begged me to send aircraft for the defence of Holland. I passed this message on to everyone concerned and went back to bed. It is not often one is rung up at that hour, and especially by a Queen. But in these days anything may happen, and far worse things too.'

Queen Wilhelmina had earlier sent a personal telegram to the King of Italy requesting him to use his influence with his political ally to save the Netherlands. He, however, was powerless, as was Pope Pius XII who, on 10th May, had sent a telegram to the Queen expressing his sympathy, for which act of charity Il Duce had reprimanded him sharply.

After his conference with the Queen, General Winkelman went to the Cabinet building. The Cabinet, on receipt of his news, considered it was high time for the Queen to depart with the utmost speed. Winkelman opposed the recommended action, considering that if the population learned that the Queen had left the country then morale would collapse so far that all resistance would evaporate. This was not the opinion of Minister Dijxhoorn, who thought it more advisable for the Queen to leave, both for her own safety and to avoid being taken prisoner and becoming a perfect hostage for the good behaviour of the Netherlands. When Dijxhoorn informed Vice-Admiral Furstner of the decision, advising him to send the rest of the fleet to Zeeland, the latter was deeply shaken. The admiral had no inkling of the seriousness of the situation and accused the ministers of contemptible defeatism, saying 'Is this the land of Tromp and De Ruyter?' The German tanks were approaching Rotterdam, Fortress Holland was under threat deep in the centre, and Winkelman wished to fight on till the last, but Dijxhoorn considered it callously irresponsible to waste more lives for a lost cause. It was imperative that the Queen leave The Hague immediately, and the Cabinet should

accompany her. Agreement was at length arrived at, and it was decided that Dijxhoorn should go to the Queen to advise her to leave. The Queen refused the minister's plea but listened to the General's arguments, and after much weighing of the pros and cons decided to take refuge in Zeeland. (Fate, however, was determined that she should go to England: a broadcast reporting the sky over Zeeland to be thick with German planes caused a diversion to Harwich, as later described. The hope that she might be able to get realistic military aid for her people if she asked for it in person helped her accept the fact that she was leaving her country.)

Meanwhile, more and more tanks of 9th Panzer Division descended on Dordrecht, together with considerable reinforcement for the Luftwaffe. The attempts to recapture the island of Dordrecht fell through completely. The night before a plan had been prepared to attack the German forces from Dordrecht to the west and from the ferry at Wieldrecht to the east, thus closing the Moerdijk-Dordrecht highway, running across the island. Unfortunately, the plan failed in practice. The detachment advancing from the Wieldrecht ferry came under incessant attack by bombers from early morning onwards, and one section of the anti-aircraft defence, which was far from superfluous, was destroyed, and the farmhouse serving as the command post for the attacking troops went up in flames. Then tanks were seen approaching from the west, bearing yellow cloth identification markers, used by the Germans to distinguish their own tanks from others, so that they would not fire on each other in error. Some of the Dutch soldiers mistook this colour for orange, and a rumour started that the French were there to give assistance. When a number of the Dutch ran enthusiastically up to the supposed Allies the first tank opened fire. Two of the tanks were destroyed and the others turned back, but heavy air

bove: The trench network of the Grebbe Line. *Below:* German attacks on Dutch
r fields were thorough – in contrast to the minimal results achieved by the
AF at Waalhaven

**General Winkelman with the army
Chief of Staff considers the course
of the invasion**

attacks dispersed the Dutch units.

The whole centre of Dordrecht was prepared for defence. All approaches were blocked with barricades and most bridges were pulled up, except those where anti-aircraft guns were positioned. In the afternoon twelve German tanks approached, but before the defenders had a chance to open fire the aide de camp of the 'unreliable' Lieutenant-Colonel Mussert came to tell them that French tanks were approaching. The Dutch started waving happily with red, white and blue flags, the first tank's crew waved back and then opened fire just in front of the bridge. That tank did not cross the bridge, and though some tanks did succeed in entering Dordrecht, where they caused tremendous havoc, they did not feel particularly secure and drove back the way they had come.

The bridges were blocked more securely and more barricades were built, but Mussert, still wielding his influence, ordered that some roads stay open for the transport of the wounded. Officers of the Bicycle Corps (sic) objected that German tanks were approaching, but he swept their criticism aside with the reply that they were seeing ghosts. The officers concluded that he was a Fifth Columnist and ignored his orders thereafter.

Ultimately Colonel van der Bijl ordered all troops to withdraw from Dordrecht over the Merwede, and when the last ferry carrying Dutch soldiers had crossed the river the boats were sunk. The troops were understandably very demoralised and many of them were coming to see Mussert as a traitor. A group of officers resolved to arrest him on suspicion. On one officer ordering him to raise his hands, he said he would not let himself be arrested by a mere captain. 'Shoot me, if you are a man,' he said, which

mark made the captain doubt if he
ere right after all, but when Mussert
sked a lieutenant who he was, and let
is hands down in the process, the
eutenant shot him and some hours
ter Lieutenant-Colonel Mussert
ied.

With the only bomber left, a T-5, the
estruction of the Moerdijk bridge
as attempted. The first bomb missed
ts target and the second did not
xplode. The bomber and an accom-
anying fighter were shot down by a
roup of Messerschmitts, and all the

**Vice-Admiral Furstner (right) was
ignorant of the extreme gravity of the
situation and opposed the suggestion
that the fleet with the Queen should
retreat to Zeeland**

crew members lost their lives. The
Moerdijk bridge had been under fire by
the Dutch artillery since the 12th, but
their task was hampered by German
bombardment. A little to the south
the Germans succeeded in crossing the
Kil, after which the village 's-Graven-
deel was set aflame. The gas-holder for

101

the village went up in flames and the spire of the church tower, containing an observation post with four men, came down. To everyone's amazement these men emerged from the rubble a quarter of an hour later unharmed.

Colonel Scharroo had given orders to prepare for the destruction of the most important bridges in Rotterdam. To be able to destroy the Willemsbrug and the railway bridge to Noorder Island, the Germans, who had been there for three days already, had first to be driven out. Lieutenant-Colonel Wilson's request for a fresh battalion under an energetic commander was granted. At 0130 on 13th May the Hunters Regiment departed from the Hook of Holland. Early in the morning the dead-tired soldiers arrived in Rotterdam. They were so exhausted that many slept sitting up with their plates of food untouched in their hands.

A farmhouse strongpoint of the Dutch forces is neutralised

The paper swastika on the Moerdijk highway is to notify German aircraft that the area is in German hands

The British Consul-General in Rotterdam insisted that the British troops who had arrived at the Hook, a Battalion of the Guards, should also go to Rotterdam as soon as possible. These were professional soldiers and were equipped with motorcycles and light armoured cars. Their commander, however, refused, because it was against the orders he had received from London. He was allowed to go to The Hague if necessary, but not to Rotterdam. And to The Hague he went, where he reported that Rotterdam was in French hands and that there was no danger whatever. Thus there was only Scharroo and his troops, who had not had a chance to sleep and had had only one square meal in four days. The marines came to their aid again, having changed their navy blue uniforms for khaki dress, in order not to

be too conspicuous. There was poor coordination between the officers leading, but one detachment reached the Boompjes (close by Willemshaven) by negotiating the ruins of burned out houses, and on its arrival was greeted by the sight of a harbour full of blazing vessels. The marines were about to position their machine-guns when they were fired on by Germans who had entrenched themselves in the building of the National Insurance Company *(Nationale Verzekerings Maatschappij)*. There were casualties and some were killed, and they were compelled to retreat but for six who became isolated on the Willemsbrug

Road blocks are demolished by the German troops

One of these was killed and another wounded, and they took shelter behind an iron sheet below road level, where they remained for more than twenty-four hours, sniping at any targets which presented themselves. The German force had been on the verge of surrender when the marines retreated.

The bid to destroy the bridges had failed.

Lieutenant-Colonel Wilson had called Headquarters during the morning to say that it was now clear that continued resistance would inevitably lead to the ultimate destruction of Rotterdam; General Winkelman replied that Rotterdam had to be defended, if necessary to the last man. When *Oberstleutnant* von Choltitz conveyed a demand for surrender to Scharroo via the Vicar of the church on Noorder Island, he therefore had to refuse. By now many parts of the town were ablaze and the streets were littered with broken glass, trams stood deserted in the highways, the British and Dutch military engineers had set fire to the oil-installations over the river near Pernis; it really seemed as if Rotterdam was going to be completely destroyed.

Near the Grebbe Line the situation was hardly better. On 12th May a regi-

The Wilhelmina Bridge, blown by the
Dutch to prevent its use by the Germans

Above: Dutch armoured cars — too few and no match for tanks
Below: Shipping ablaze in Rotterdam harbour

Above: Rotterdam's streets fill with smoke . *Below:* The oil-storage tanks at Pernis set on fire by the British and Dutch to deny their contents to the Wehrmacht

ment of the SS had penetrated deeply into the Grebbe Line and if they succeeded in breaking through near Rhenen the whole area would be lost and the Dutch would have to retreat behind the New Dutch Water Line (*Nieuwe Hollandse Waterlinie*). The Dutch troops here were almost useless because of lack of sleep and it was vitally important that they be replaced by fresh soldiers. Replacements were long overdue. When at last reinforcements came they were immediately engaged by infantry of the 207th Infantry Division, which had replaced the SS Standarte. There was heavy

firing but the Dutch line held until in some sections the ammunition ran out and the defenders could do nothing but surrender. These local failures were sufficient to allow the Germans in some places to break through the Stop Line and take other sectors in the rear. Not a few fled in panic, and very often prisoners were used by the Germans as shields to force the Dutch to surrender. From the diary of a Dutch soldier one learns how he was confronted by two rows of Germans each with a Dutch soldier in front of them. The prisoners cried to their comrades not to shoot but to sur

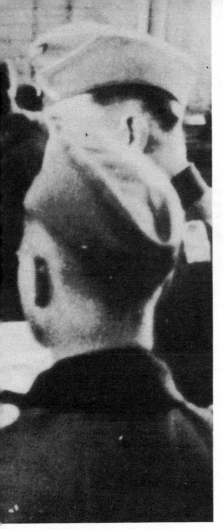

Landzaat was accompanied by a few officers and men and their armament consisted of one light machine-gun, a number of rifles and revolvers and very little ammunition. They set the machine-gun up on a table and fired through the window. The Germans, however, soon brought up a heavy artillery piece and the pavilion started to crumble. The major was wounded and he ordered his men to leave by way of the trenches behind the building, but he himself stayed. The pavilion was shot to ruins and the major died still fighting.

Thanks to a few who, like Major Landzaat, decided to fight on come what might, the Grebbe Line did not fall earlier. Lieutenant-Colonel Hennink's action is another example. Hennink had prevented the men of a battalion which had come to the Grebbe Line as reinforcement, from running away. His command post, in the woods north-east of the viaduct, was undergoing intensive shelling and there were many dead and wounded. The adjutant standing to one side of the Lieutenant-Colonel was hit in the back by shell fragments, and when the soldier standing on Hennink's other side was required to fetch medical aid he remarked dryly that he also was wounded and drew attention to one of his eyes which was hanging out of its socket; notwithstanding his fearful injury he helped the adjutant to the doctor before seeking treatment for himself. By no means all were as courageous as this soldier. Most of the men who had been transferred from other units were completely demoralised and cowered in corners of the trenches, from where they were chased by Hennink and assigned to positions with a special patrol which had orders to shoot them if they attempted to run away. That helped. Towards evening the Lieutenant-

ender. Many of the Dutch soldiers ignored the invitation and continued firing, till one of the prisoners suddenly clutched his stomach and fell, probably hit by his own people.

To set against examples of cowardice in the Dutch army there were many instances in which great courage was shown.

When the command post of the 1st Battalion was surrounded, Major Landzaat, the commander, decided to fight to the end. They had commandeered a small restaurant of the *Ouwehands Dierenpark* (the Rhenen Zoo), a small thin-walled building.

111

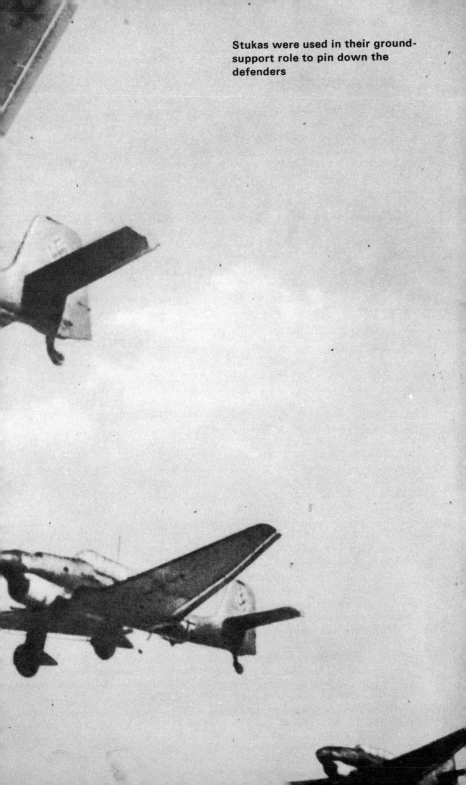

Stukas were used in their ground-support role to pin down the defenders

Colonel handed over the regimental colours to a sergeant and a private who were to take them to Fortress Holland. Their mission succeeded. It was discovered subsequently that two of the three commanders of the 8th regiment were killed, together with 180 other officers and men. The German infantry had still not succeeded in crossing the railway. In the morning the SS attackers had tried to deceive the defenders of the viaduct by donning Dutch uniforms. The attempt failed because they were still wearing the easily recognizable German boots. Then the Luftwaffe came to their aid with twenty-seven Stukas but the defenders, under Captain Gelderman, with two lieutenants, two state policemen (Marechaussees) and a few others who refilled the magazines of the two machine-guns and served the single anti-tank gun, stayed at their post. Finally, at 1330, one of Gelderman's group succeeded in blowing up the viaduct after working all morning

to place the explosives under heavy fire.

In the afternoon the German troops were fired on by a Dutch battalion which had had to make its way to the railway against a steady stream of refugees. At that the Germans abandoned the wood-working factory where they had been esconced, because artillery reinforcements had been ordered to shell the Dutch defended railway. They were quite unaware that Gelderman's group was completely out of ammunition; in fact they thought that heavy Dutch resistance had still to be broken. Actually the Dutch defence had completely fallen apart since about noon. The morale of the Dutch troops was above all undermined by the constant heavy artillery fire to which they were exposed without themselves ever getting a glimpse of the Germans. Nervousness increased with reports of the approach of the German infantry, and a number of badly affected soldiers ran away and

moment crossed the rails and the barbed wire of the railroad.

At other sectors of the Grebbe Line the situation was much better. The 2nd Division of IV Army Corps received excellent artillery support (in contrast to the case of 4th Division, where much was left to be desired). Dutch bombardment was so effective that the Germans assumed that civilians were exchanging telephone messages with observers hidden in the terrain. The entire population of Ede was evacuated by the Germans to prevent this. Only towards the evening did the Germans succeed in taking a few points on the outposts strip, but the main defence line was still intact.

There was some success also at the Betuwe position where A Brigade in the morning repulsed an attack by about 200 Germans at the Waal (a tributary of the Rhine) and in the afternoon drove back six boats attempting the crossing, of which two were sunk. In the evening they tried to blow up the railway bridge near Rhenen, but the demolition charges refused to detonate. Artillery fire was directed at the site of the explosives under the structure and the last available projectile succeeded; the bridge was destroyed.

The only clear-cut breakthrough the the Germans achieved was near Rhenen, but that was enough, for if the Grebbe Line was broken at one point the whole line had to be abandoned. The IV and the II Army Corps, B Brigade and A Brigade, all would have to fall back on the eastern boundary of Fortress Holland, behind the New Dutch Water Line. The Line was in fact hardly a barrier at all. The assumption was that large areas of water would halt the German advance, but no one had predicted the low water level of the rivers (because of the very dry weather that spring) and that it would take a considerable time for the polders to be inundated once the

were fired on by a squadron of the hussars. The squadron commander informed his regimental commander that the danger existed of his regiment being surrounded and, the commanders having no idea how many troops were actually present, decided to retreat to Elst. All the time desertion was becoming more frequent. Captain Gelderman, sending an aide with a request for food for 600 men (many had had nothing to eat for days) altered the number to 400 when he learned that 200 men had deserted. It appeared that only fifteen men had stuck to the positions originally assigned them.

The fleeing and panic-stricken soldiers were dive-bombed and shelled to the point where their officers could exert no authority over them; moreover in many cases the officers had no idea where to contact their superiors because the command posts had been changed two or three times. Nevertheless, not one German had up to that

sluices were opened. The evacuation of the 23,000 inhabitants of the area with their cattle, 60,000 animals, went ahead smoothly, but at night most of the fields were still dry. The retreating troops suspected that traitors were directing the operation. In addition to the failure of the *Nieuwe Hollandse Water Linie*, the eastern boundary of Fortress Holland was almost without fortification; there were no trenches, no bunkers, no machine-gun posts, no telephone communications. Furthermore, the troops who had the task of defending had for the most part never been in the area before; for them it was totally unknown territory, a considerable handicap.

On the whole, however, the retreat itself went quite satisfactorily. Small groups were sometimes taken but by great good luck the Luftwaffe was inactive during this time. The heavy fog patches which hung low over the land during the early morning formed a very welcome shelter.

General Winkelman gave orders to form a wide anti-tank barrier around The Hague. The Hague itself was further reinforced with a strong guard on all the bridges. The navy's defence of the IJsselmeer was marked by an ominous lack of success; the gunboat *Friso* was so heavily damaged by air attack that she had to be scuttled.

Incoming messages at Headquarters

The Gunboat *Friso,* before her fatal trip

were all, without exception, extremely sombre. Not without reason did General Winkelman and Major-General van Voorst tot Voorst regard the situation as very critical. But the German Generals were not satisfied either. They had expected resistance to come to an end on the 10th. As yet they were unaware that the Dutch troops behind the eastern front had withdrawn to Fortress Holland, and assumed that quelling resistance would not be an easy task. They were also apprehensive of possible British assistance via IJmuiden, and it was chiefly for this reason that General von Küchler was ordered to take Fortress Holland as soon as possible.

He demanded that on the 14th the entire Grebbe Line must be broken through, and that 9th Panzer Division of XXXIV Army Corps under General Schmidt were to cross the Dordrecht-Rotterdam line and proceed from there to Utrecht. After that Amsterdam had to be taken, to prevent the Dutch army withdrawing to northern Holland. The German troops who had tried to land in Noord-Holland by way of the IJsselmeer were still stranded at Kornwerderzand, where the defence was still going strong.

But the tanks had first to cross the

117

Maas at Rotterdam, and there the defence continued to be tough and persistent. Hitler sent his generals instructions, which they received on 14th May, to break the unexpectedly strong resistance in the shortest possible time. For this purpose the full strength of the Luftwaffe would be available. That night General Schmidt received orders from Küchler. He was to break resistance in Rotterdam by whatever means proved necessary, up to and including the destruction of the town.

Meanwhile Queen Wilhelmina was on her way to England. At 1000 her car left The Hague for the Hook of Holland. The journey took over an hour, and the Queen hardly escaped death when a German bomb exploded near the car. They sailed on the *Herewaard* for Zeeland but had to change course because of mines and air raids, so Harwich became their destination. At 1700 the *Herewaard* docked at Harwich, where a special train was waiting to bring the Queen to London. King George and Queen Elizabeth were at the station to welcome her, as were the Dutch Ambassador and Ministers van Kleffens and Welter, to whom she said 'We must start work at once'. The King offered her hospitality in Buckingham Palace. 'With deep reluctance she was persuaded to accept the inevitable', wrote the King, who had never met her before, in his diary. 'She was naturally very upset and had brought no clothes with her.'

Queen Wilhelmina started work immediately. She had a discussion with van Kleffens lasting some hours

Below left: General Kuchler. The general had orders to take Fortress Holland with the utmost speed, before further intervention by the British. At the Kornwerderzand resistance stayed strong. *Right:* A Dutch soldier on a mine laying mission before the withdrawal, and, *Below:* the Dutch ensured that no transport would be left in a usable condition

Queen Wilhelmina broadcasts messages of hope to her people all over the world from London

and she was, as he recorded later, 'shocked and tense, but totally in control of herself, absolutely not despondent, determined and able to think sharply and clearly'. A telegram was sent to the French President, Lebrun, pressing for aid: if more help was not forthcoming, General Winkelman would have no choice but to capitulate. It was also decided that van Kleffens should go again with a similar request to Churchill. The Prime Minister was already asleep, but they were received by the Chief of the Military Cabinet, Sir Harold Ismay, in the War Room under the Cabinet Office. (This War Room, containing Churchill's private suite, still exists – forty feet down under King Charles Street and George Street, protected

King George VI of Great Britain and Queen Elizabeth. The King and Queen welcomed Queen Wilhelmina and provided her with accommodation at Buckingham Palace

by thirty feet of solid concrete.) Lieutenant-Colonel van de Plassche painted the situation in the Netherlands and van Kleffens gave a brief outline of essential requirements: 'The possibilities in the Netherlands are the following: Firstly, effective help should at once be rendered, in which case effective resistance can be carried on. Secondly, if effective help is not given, the General, Commander-in-Chief, will be empowered to act as he deems fit, having regard to the military forces and the civilian population,'

Ismay and Douglas, Deputy Chief of the Air Staff, invited by Ismay to be present at the meeting, thought this to be a fair statement, though both of them knew how impossible it was for Britain to offer any help at all; they had not even tried to wake Churchill.

121

Ultimatum and destruction

he following morning the Dutch
earned from radio broadcasts that the
ueen had left her country. Most of
ne people in Holland felt deeply
efeated by the news. Foreign broad-
asts during the night had already
iven the news that the Dutch Queen
ad arrived in London, and especially
mong the military this information
as taken to mean that all was lost,
nd they felt deserted. An attempt was
ade to boost morale by issuing the
ollowing proclamation:

'The military situation can be
egarded as follows:

In the northern provinces the enemy
ave secured themselves. An attempt
o force through the Afsluitdijk has
p till now not been successful. The
northern part of Rotterdam is securely
in our hands. The army has this past
night withdrawn to our well-known
New Dutch Water Line. The position
of Den Helder is totally intact. In
Brabant the situation is not clear.
Zeeland is securely in our hands. Our
air defences, notwithstanding losses,
remain prepared. The fight is hard.
But it is a worthwhile fight because it
concerns our independent existence
which we gained centuries ago under
the leadership of Oranje.

Long live Her Majesty the Queen!

Long live the fatherland!'

After this communication had been
broadcast a message was received at
Headquarters from the garrison commander of Rotterdam. He had received
an ultimatum to surrender within two
hours or the city would be totally destroyed. The opening artillery bombardment would begin at 1300, followed
twenty minutes later by the Luftwaffe's bombers, after which the
German troops would cross the river,
supported by tanks and flame-
throwers, to march upon Gouda and
Utrecht, and to Overschie and The
Hague. As a concession Choltitz would
allow the female inhabitants of
Noorder Island and the male citizens
of under sixteen and over sixty years
of age to cross the Koninginnebrug to
Rotterdam-Zuid. If the Dutch accepted the ultimatum the bombers
would be notified by red Verey lights
and the raid would be cancelled.

Much precious time was wasted
because the ultimatum was not signed.
At the foot appeared merely 'The
Commander of the German Troops'.
Wilson thought it a worthless document and said as much to General
Winkelman. Colonel Scharroo saw no
reason to surrender; that very morning he had sent all the available anti-
tank guns to the Willemsbrug and
prepared the destruction of the railway viaduct at Beurs station. There
were no Germans north of the river

**Where the old city stood before May
1940**

123

and according to him the ultimatum was nothing more than a scrap of rubbish. But the final decision had to come from the C-in-C. At 1145 Scharroo received word from Headquarters that the ultimatum could only be taken seriously if it was signed properly. At 1210 Scharroo sent a note to '*Der Oberst-Kommandant der Truppen in Rotterdam*'. This letter reached Choltitz only fifteen minutes before the time the ultimatum was due to expire. General Schmidt was of the opinion that the people of Rotterdam were ready to negotiate, otherwise they would not have replied to the ultimatum at all, and he gave orders to postpone the firing and composed a radio message in which he stated that the bombing of Rotterdam would be delayed by one hour. It was by then twelve noon and half the bombers had already taken off from their base for their one-and-a-half hours' flight to Rotterdam. They had instructions, as stated in the ultimatum, that they

should cancel the mission if red Verey lights were shot over Noorder Island. But General Student had lost half his radio equipment during the artillery bombardment of Waalhaven and he had difficulty in getting through – so more precious time was lost. Schmidt received no news from Germany and assumed that the bombers were not going to arrive. When Choltitz read Scharroo's reply he warned his commander, General Student. The latter went with his superior, General Schmidt and the commanding general of 9th Panzer Division, by car to Captain Backer, who had conveyed Scharroo's answer to Choltitz. On the back of Scharroo's letter Schmidt wrote that it was required that the German troops be allowed to march into Rotterdam by daylight north of the river, and that *die tapferen holländische Truppen* (the courageous Dutch troops) lay down their arms, their officers being allowed to retain theirs. Backer said that Colonel

Scharroo would again contact Headquarters and, if Headquarters agreed, all troops on the long Maas front would be warned, but time was needed for this. Schmidt was prepared to grant three hours; he signed with his name and rank and added *Kommandierender General eines Armee-Korps* (Commanding General of an Army Corps). A few minutes later, from the south and east, some hundred German bombers roared in.

General Schmidt, who had assumed that his order to postpone the raid had reached the base concerned, cried out: *'Um Gotteswillen, das gibt eine Katastrophe! Mein Gott, mein Gott, was wirdt jetzt geschehen? Das wird ein zweites Warschau!'* (God Almighty, there will be a catastrophe! My God, my God, what will happen? It will be a second Warsaw!)

The red Verey lights shot into the air; Schmidt had some bales of cotton rolled into the street from a department store, but it was already too late.

The leader of the wave approaching from the south saw the Verey lights and turned away with his planes, but the first three machines had already released their bombs. The greater part of the bombing force proceeded to carry out their mission. In Rotterdam people fled into the cellars or threw themselves flat in the streets if they could not reach a house in time – the rare German soldier included.

Soon the air was full of the howl of air-raid warning sirens, the rumbling drone of the bombers, the scream of falling bombs and the thuds of the first explosions.

Rotterdam now experienced those scenes of carnage and devastation which, starting with Guernica, continued on both sides on ever more horrific scale up to the fire raids on Tokyo and the final acts of the Second

Heinkel IIIs leave their base. The signal that the mission was cancelled, came too late to prevent catastrophe

Above: The great fire develops. *Below:* The fire at its height

World War, the nuclear attacks on Hiroshima and Nagasaki.

In one cellar under a small shop at the Oostplein more than thirty men, women and children were jammed together so tightly that when the rear of the cellar was hit by a bomb the unscathed were powerless to do anything for the wounded, whose groaning was punctuated by the sound of further explosions. The water mains were hit, gas pipes and the power network were destroyed, the telephone system ceased to function. The huge fountains from the broken water pipes subsided once the pressure was lost, and of course were no longer available when water was needed most.

A new wave of bombs fell. The Bijenkorf department store, the Municipal Hospital, the Police Headquarters, the De Doelen building, the Fire Brigade Headquarters, the temporary Raampoort hospital and the penitentiary at the Noordsingel – where the inmates were set free – were all hit. From De Doelen a large number of interned Germans and NSB members fled into the street, injuring their hands on the barbed wire. From burning buildings people came running with their clothing alight, to die horribly in the street. The fire brigade could not be reached because the telephones did not work; not that this circumstance was of importance as the Brigade building itself was a ruin, the roads were blocked at intervals by rubble and of course the water supply had been effectively cut off. Some firemen attempted to extinguish the fires on their own initiative but their efforts were hardly significant in the gigantic conflagration which was developing. Splinters of burning wood and sparks were drifting in the air, setting fire to curtains waving in the wind through the shattered windows (most windows were broken by bomb blast) and starting fires in otherwise undamaged houses; and there was a strong west wind which was spreading the fire at high speed.

After the raid the Coolsingel was ablaze on all sides, and the crisp noise of the spreading fire and the thud of falling rubble sounded loud in the quiet after the bombing. The dangerous animals in the Diergaarde Blijdorp (the Zoo) had been killed on the 12th, and when the bombing started all the other cages were opened, to give the animals some chance of survival in case the zoo was hit as well.

The people who came out of their shelters were numb with shock. Everything around them seemed aflame, and it was difficult to breathe with the sharp smoke irritating throat and nose. In the streets and in the burning houses themselves there were heartbreaking sights. In front of one house six corpses were lying scattered over the pavement – an entire family – and in another ruin a small boy was hanging head down, clamped between fallen beams; not able to free himself he must have seen the fire creeping towards him. In another place a child's hand was protruding from the rubble, then one would see a human body plastered against the surface of a door, and another hanging out of a window.

Most of the survivors fled this devastation as quickly as they could; the heat alone was unbearable. At various times after the bombing people were found who had not been able to get away. There was a butcher who had sought shelter in his refrigerator and three women who had taken cover in a vault. The doors had buckled and they had suffocated, unable to free themselves. Emergency rescue teams were feverishly digging in rubble heaps hoping to find survivors. Sometimes people dug their own way out of the rubble: those who survived the bomb in the cellar beneath the shop at Oostplein, for example; clearing the stairs of the larger debris, to hasten their escape, one encountered something soft. It proved to be the squashed head of a young girl. Eventually they cleared a narrow opening sufficient for the

The rubble of Rotterdam

thinnest man of the group to force himself through, but then the tunnel collapsed again. Late in the afternoon the remainder were discovered by a member of the auxiliary fire brigade. Covered with blood from the glass splinters which were everywhere, they emerged from the rubble heap to see the sun at last – a burning red ball through the clouds of dust.

The fire at the hospital was uncontrollable and the only solution was to evacuate all the patients. Men straight from the operating theatre were helping; people were brought in from the street to lend a hand. The patients were brought over to the Catholic church where there was an emergency hospital, and when that was full other patients were taken to the Laurenskerk. Both these churches caught fire before long and again the patients had to be found somewhere to go – almost an impossibility for no-

where was there safety; the whole centre of the town was afire.

The conflagration crept further and further east, block after block of houses succumbing to the flames. No preventive action was of the slightest use. People took what they could easily carry, sometimes merely a piece of cheese or a loaf, and fled. Many slept in the open that night because they did not dare go into a house after the horror they had gone through. Thousands had gone into the Kralingerhout, a wood just outside Rotterdam, where the whole night through people were wandering to and fro calling the names of their relatives. Sometimes they found their parents or their children whom they had supposed dead, but as often their search was fruitless.

During the evening the wind had changed and was now blowing strongly from the east, spreading the fire westward to parts of the town which up till then had seemed safe. A great glare hung over the burning city.

In the afternoon people on Betuwe had seen the sun strangely obscured, as in an eclipse, and now with the coming of evening they saw the frightening fireglow in the direction of the great harbour town many miles away. The city appeared to be one enormous sea of fire, and the sky was a hot crimson blotched with purple. Gigantic smoke columns poured up, taking with them the lighter fragments of the wreckage, still burning. Heavy explosions occurred, after each of which clouds of sparks and flames leapt high into the sky. Nobody could go into that inferno; the fire had to be allowed to consume everything.

The morning after the holocaust one of the fugitives returned to the town to see if there was anything at all remaining. It took him many hours. When he finally came back, late in the afternoon, there were tears pouring down his face, and all he could say was: 'Our Rotterdam does not exist any more. Nothing is left.'

From all the surrounding towns and villages and even from Delft, The Hague, Leyden, Haarlem, Amsterdam, and Wormerveer, the fire brigades came. By 15th May the fires were contained and a day later the largest and most threatening fires had been extinguished. Many firemen had been working more than twenty-four hours at a stretch, climbing and descending stairs, climbing over heaps of rubble, continually encountering the bodies of those who had perished. It was a long time before the fire was completely conquered in those parts which had suffered most, and small fires were continually breaking out in the smouldering debris. At the Haringvliet, ruins of warehouses containing peas were still smouldering ten weeks later, but the tobacco stocks took the longest; it was mid-August before the last flame was extinguished.

While the destruction of Rotterdam was in its opening stages the military on both sides were still in the midst of the confusion generated by conflicting motives and the disastrous breakdown of communication. Captain Backer, who had received the second ultimatum from General Schmidt at 1315, had not even reached the north end of the Willemsbrug before the bombs began to fall. The two German officers accompanying him took to their heels. The journey to Colonel Scharroo's Headquarters in Blijdorp took the Captain forty-five minutes, for he had to go straight through the centre of the town where the great fire was developing, and the Colonel was at his wits' end when Backer arrived. The second ultimatum proved very difficult to read, but one thing was certain – surrender was demanded and this had to be offered before 1620. It was hard for the Colonel to come to a decision. Both Mayor Oud and Alderman Brautigam strongly advised him to surrender; had not one German bombing been enough? Wasn't it clear as daylight that Rotterdam would be annihilated completely unless the fighting was halted? Would more innocent victims have to suffer? Lieutenant-Colonel Wilson remained silent. Scharroo's most difficult problem was that telephone communication could no longer be made with General Headquaters and he doubted that he would be able to get instructions in time to be of any use. Rotterdam was in chaos and the military situation seemed hopeless. Backer, who had not believed that German tanks had reached Rotterdam, had now seen them with his own eyes. How could the colonel and his worn-out troops resist with any hope of success? Scharroo felt the weight of a heavy responsibility, for if he capitulated he would open wide the door to Fortress Holland. He was not at this time aware (and neither was General Winkelman) that if Rotterdam refused to surrender the same fate would befall Utrecht, The Hague, Amsterdam and Haarlem. This knowledge would undoubtedly have helped him to decide.

In the midst of the deliberations

Wilson said suddenly: 'Colonel, I am
here as proxy for the Commander-in-
Chief. On behalf of the Commander-
in-Chief I ask you what decision you
take, cut off from your superiors'.
'Capitulate', was the answer. 'Taking
into account', Wilson went on, 'that
communications with our superiors
have broken down, and that all means
of defence are now at an end, I declare
as deputy of the Commander-in-Chief
that I approve your decision and take
responsibility thereof upon myself.'
It was then just after 1430. Together
with the two officers who had accompanied him, Wilson jumped into a car
and drove to The Hague. They could
not take the direct route because,
despite the nature of Wilson's mission
he would certainly have been delayed
– or even shot in error – by the Germans at Overschie. They went north
instead . . . and encountered an anti-

**Firemen working to quench the last
fires**

ank barricade at Bleiswijk, close by the Gouden-The Hague highway, and could not proceed. They left the car, climbed over the barricade, and continued their journey by truck.

Colonel Scharroo had decided not to risk delay and, though he had until 1620 before the deadline was reached, he and Backer arrived at Noorder Island well before 1600. At precisely 1500 he had signed an order directing his sub-commander to cease fire and wait for further instructions. On the second German ultimatum Scharroo had written only one word: *Angenommen* (accepted), signing it with his name and adding his rank and function. On joining the generals Schmidt and Student, and the commander of the tank division in a car on the Island, Scharroo, who on his way had seen the devastation of Rotterdam with his own eyes, gave vent to his deep indignation and accused General

Schmidt of breaking his word. The General replied: '*Ich verstehe, Herr Oberst, das Sie bitter sind*' (I understand your bitterness, Commander), and he declared that he deplored the bombing and had done his best to prevent it.

Other matters remained to be taken care of. Schmidt required all Dutch troops to be south of the river before dusk, after which, at 1910, the German forces would march into the burning city. The colonel asked to be permitted to return immediately to make sure the order reached the Dutch troops in time, but the city was now such an inferno that he did not reach his headquarters until 1830. By this time German bombers were on their way to Rotterdam for the second time, on Göring's orders; the Luftwaffe chief was impatient with the length of time capitulation talks seemed to be taking. Sponeck's division at Overschie was to be relieved, Rotterdam to be bombed again and the tanks to break through to Overschie immediately. Kesselring prepared a radio

Above: Göring visits the scene of destruction wrought by his airmen. He became anxious at the time capitulation negotiations were taking place and ordered a further and superfluous bombing. *Below:* The port under the pall of its own burning

ssage, making clear that it was not
s idea: '*Feldmarschall befehlt noch
ute ohne Rücksicht auf kapitulation
rchbruch zu Sponeck. Kampfge-
wader angreift zwischen 19 und 20
r mit drie Gruppen und wirft Bomben
nn ich nicht sofort Meldung über
ginnen Durchbruch erhalte.*' Thus the
cond bombardment would take place
tween 1720 and 1820 (Dutch time).
Most probably the Heinkels had left
eir base at 1530. General Schmidt
1 not waste time in coding – at 1715
cabled 'in clear' '*Nordteil Rotterdam
setzt*' (North of Rotterdam taken),
1ich was not true yet, '*Keine Bomben
rfen*' (Do not drop bombs). This
ply was luckily effective and the
:inkels, already very near Rotter-
m, were ordered back to their base.
The German Ambassador, interned
the Hotel des Indes in The Hague,
as informed of the capitulation of
1e Dutch Army, but it was em-
1asized that Zeeland and the Marines
d not capitulate and neither did the
utch Government.

The Royal Navy and the Dutch
erchant Fleet departed for England
d the Dutch Cabinet moved to
ndon. Thus ended five days of
1equal combat and began the five
ng years of German occupation.

At the German Legation in the Hotel
s Indes they heard ammunition ex-
oding, and an immediate demand
as made to cease the destruction of
ar material. In consequence the
ermans got the Artillery Establish-
ent at the Hembrug – the largest
eapon and ammunition factory in
1e Netherlands – totally undamaged.
employed more than 7,000 workers
d the industry had been thoroughly
odernised not long before, and
1ough in comparison with the muni-
ons works in Germany it was only a
1all enterprise, it undeniably contri-
ited to the might of the Wehrmacht.
Most of the air force left, together
ith the flying instructors in their
ainers, for Britain. Winkelman was
ld to ensure that the personnel of
1e naval air force, who had gone to

Britain, would not continue fighting.
If they were taken prisoner they
would be considered *franc-tireurs* and
shot. Winkelman replied to the German general that he could not comply,
since only that part of the Dutch
Army present in the Netherlands was
subject to the conditions of the
armistice and that the Netherlands
as such were still in a state of war with
Germany. All Dutch troops outside
the Netherlands, and especially those
in the Netherlands East Indies, would
fight on, being outside Winkelman's
jurisdiction.

The agreement was signed by von
Küchler for Germany and Winkelman
for the Netherlands. The fighting,
except in Zeeland, was over. It was
about ten in the morning. Hitler was
informed and he ordered that the 9th
Panzer Division and the SS Leibstandarte Adolf Hitler were to enter
Amsterdam and The Hague immediately. In the German press a proclamation by the Führer was printed
thanking the German soldiers for their
defeat of *eine starke wohlvorbereitere
Armee die sich hinter fast unüberwind-
lich erscheinenden Hindernissen und
militärische Befestigungen zähe ver-
teidigte* (a strong and well prepared
army who had defended themselves
behind sheer unconquerable obstacles). The heroic effort of the
parachutists and airborne troops
'resolute in the face of death' he
selected for special mention. The
German papers were directed to
increase criticism of the Dutch
Cabinet and to use Prince Bernhard
in cartoons, but not, however, to
mention Queen Wilhelmina. Princess
Juliana too had to be respected.

By 11th May a start had already
been made on towing ships still under
construction for the Dutch Navy to
England, a task needing some courage;
slowly traversing the North Sea without escort in 1940 was dangerous work.
Two new submarines, the 021 and 022,
arrived in one piece in England,
though without torpedoes. Not having
charts they used an old German

fishery map which they had acquired
from a coaster in Flushing. Two other
submarines, the 023 and the 024, were
still lying at the wharf in Rotterdam
when the Germans attacked, but still
attempted a getaway. The 024 had
never even dived before. The biggest
risk was the magnetic mines in the
Nieuwe Waterweg, and the German
planes which had sunk the *Van Galen*
on 10th May had to be taken into
account too. One boat, loaded with the
gold of the Netherlands Bank in
Rotterdam, had already suffered from
a magnetic mine. Two courageous
pilots offered to bring the 023 and 024
to the open sea, sailing outside the
fairway, as near as possible to the
bank of the river. When night fell they
departed, being shot at by Dutch
troops who did not understand what
was going on. During the night they
made good progress, but when dawn
came both submarines dived to wait
for dusk. For the 024 this presented

Utrecht capitulates

oblems. The ship leaked badly and, ing full of cork and other rubbish ɔm the wharf, the pumps became ɔgged and they had to surface again. it they too arrived safely in England, .thout the benefit of charts and their ly signalling apparatus an ordinary ectric torch. The Naval Attaché in ɔndon had ships but no personnel, so e cabled Admiral Furstner request-g the necessary experts, which the ɩvy supplied. For the most part the utch navy was in Indian waters, and r them the battle would go on as ɩough the capitulation had not taken ace.

The remainder of the planes of the aval Air Force were flown to Cher-ɔurg and Brest, and by 17th May venty-five planes with their crews ɩd other personnel had escaped.

That so much of the navy went to ɩgland was considered by the army

to be nothing but desertion. Admiral Furstner, however, was of the opinion that though it was very unpleasant that a part of the Dutch Kingdom was lost, there were still the Dutch East Indies and Surinam and the Antilles to be considered, and the complete merchant fleet was in England and would require escorts. The Admiral consulted his deputy about what would be the best thing for him to do, and the deputy gave it as his opinion that the Admiral and as many naval officers as could should join the Dutch vessels now in England. Furst-ner called Winkelman to inform him of his decision and did not receive a very friendly reaction. The Admiral asked Winkelman for a summary of the situation, and when Winkelman told him how bad it was Furstner remarked that he thought it was probably the last time he would hear his voice. In the meantime the French general Mittelhauser, together with three French officers, arrived at The

Hague on 14th May, having been sent there as a delegation by General Gamelin. When he had had the situation explained to him he reacted with the words: '*Vous n'allez pas nous laissez ici dans cette sourciere. Je vous prie.de me procurer les moyens de quitter la Hollande au plus vite.*' (You are not going to leave me in this whirlpool. I would appreciate you helping me to leave Holland as soon as possible.) Admiral Furstner's party was therefore enlarged to include the French delegation. It was considered too obvious to sail off in the Schevening lifeboat, as had been suggested, and they therefore embarked on a fishing boat, the *Johanna,* and shaped their course for Dunkirk. Off the French coast they were swooped at from all sides by boats which gave every sign of being about to fire on them, but the sight of Mittelhauser standing in the bows, wearing his red képi, changed hostility to a hearty welcome. Furstner and his staff later succeeded in reaching England unharmed.

At about 1545 General Student's Flieger-Division had started to cross the Maas bridges. An hour later they were followed by the SS Leibstandarte Adolf Hitler. Towards the evening the SS division reached Sponeck's fighting troops at Overschie. Student and Choltitz were in Scharroo's Headquarters talking about the particulars of the surrender. Mayor Oud was present at the meeting which took

The Dutch Navy scuttles those of its ships which could not reach the comparative safety of England

place in a room at the front of the first floor. Suddenly there was the noise of gunfire. Student recognized by the sound that the shots came from German rifles, and hurried to the window to investigate. By a gross coincidence he was hit by a stray bullet and fell. Hundreds of Dutch soldiers and civilians were at that moment waiting in front of the building and at the shout of *Student ist erschossen* (Student has been shot) excited German soldiers grabbed them, ordered them into rows with Dutch officers they had dragged from Headquarters, placed machine-guns in position and would most probably have proceeded to mass execution had not Choltitz intervened. He ordered

all the people who had been about to be shot to be escorted quickly to the nearby church, pending the result of investigation. (Later it was shown that German weapons had made the bullet holes in the Headquarters wall.) Mayor Oud had immediately arranged for Student to be rushed to the hospital at the Bergweg where he was operated upon successfully. But the German troops had been made so apprehensive that many of them did not dare drink tapwater, for fear of being poisoned. Oud was required to send out a proclamation, stating that

137

he would guarantee the safety of the invaders with his own life and that the Germans were there as friends. He acceded to the first statement but refused to give his name to the second, and on the proclamation (printed on a handpress for there was no electricity) no more was stated than that the German troops had been ordered to treat the Dutch population with respect. Oud, for his part, would do his utmost to defend and advance all the lawful interests of the population *vis-à-vis* the occupying army.

When Wilson finally arrived at Headquarters his first words to Major-General van Voorst tot Voorst were 'General, I come from hell'. He retailed what he had seen of the destruction in Rotterdam and reported that he had authorized Colonel Scharroo to surrender. At first Winkelman thought that the capitulation of Rotterdam, though a calamity, was an isolated

Kuchler and General Bock meet at The Hague to finalize the surrender

Netherlands troops in England inspected by a visiting US offical

setback. New defence lines had been built up and he hoped that Fortress Holland could be maintained. In the course of the afternoon, however, Utrecht received an ultimatum; like the Rotterdam document, its message was: surrender or be totally destroyed. In accordance with Winkelman's orders to fight to the last man, the ultimatum was rejected, but the Luftwaffe dropped 4,000 pamphlets over the town threatening it with the same fate as Warsaw if it did not surrender. The Utrecht commander informed GHQ and it at last became clear to everyone what lay in store for the Netherlands if resistance was maintained. Fortress Holland was still intact and could probably be defended for a considerable time, but where would be the profit if all the towns were destroyed meanwhile and the Netherlands as a whole were devas-

tated? But before the nation's surrender was officially transmitted to the victor there was much to be done. The navy was given the task of rendering all the harbours and port installations unusable. All military archives had to be burned in the incinerators of the refuse centre in The Hague and van Oorschot, Head of the Dutch Secret Service, also had many documents, in particular lists of names, which could not be allowed to fall into German hands; the Ministry of Defence's secret files were destroyed and weapons were smashed, sunk in the sea or stripped of vital parts. In their zeal those who were given the job of destroying papers also destroyed *Directions for Time of Occupation,* but forgot to burn the files of the Topographical Service, which proved of great value to the Germans. Finally, the text of the radio announcement informing the Dutch population of the defeat had to be prepared.

The two completed new Dutch submarines 021 *(above)* and 022 *(below)* which found their way to England with an old coaster's fishing map. *Right:* The 023 which, with 024, escaped though still untested. The 024 had never even dived prior to her journey to England.

Occupation

The Mayors of Amsterdam, The Hague and other big cities, where the Germans were due to march triumphantly in, asked the citizens to maintain quietness and order, the mark of Holland's old civilization, and by and large the population showed restraint and dignity in this difficult time.

The Fuhrer honoured the German troops in the Netherlands with the words:

'In five days you have attacked, broken the air defences and in the end forced the surrender of a strong well-prepared army defending itself bravely behind seemingly unbeatable obstacles and receiving military reinforcements. With that you have accomplished a stroke which is unique. The future will show its military significance. Only through your exemplary co-ordination, through determined leadership and the courage of the soldiers, especially through the brave performance of the airborne troops with their contempt for death, has this success been possible. On behalf of the German people I thank you and express my admiration for you.'

This was a sample of Hitler's rhetoric to which the Dutch became used during the following five years.

Meanwhile a notice appeared in all the newspapers; the Mayor of Rotterdam requested everybody who did not have to be in Rotterdam for urgent reasons to stay away for the time being. People wanting information about relatives should direct their inquiries to the Children's Police Department, housed in the Oostervantstraat police station in Rotterdam, Telephone 35888.

People worked desperately hard to

The Hague. Germans and Dutch National Socialists proclaim the conquest

bring some order out of the chaos created during the five days of battle, and then there was the problem of trying to take up everyday life again. It was not easy to forget that during these five days about twenty-five hundred soldiers and the same number of civilians had lost their lives.

The many prohibitions began to pile up: it was forbidden to possess carrier-pigeons, all had to be killed within a week; the Boy Scouts were forbidden, because the movement had originated in Britain; menus in restaurants could no longer be presented in the French language, but only in Dutch and German, except in the case of Indonesian, Chinese and Italian restaurants. The mayors of most towns were replaced one after the other by NSB members, without reference to their training or abilities. Inevitably, but most serious of all, the German Command ordered

Mayor Oud greets a German general. The atmosphere became more and more strained with time

A German military band entertains at Scheveningen. Efforts such as this to mollify the Dutch petered out as the war progressed

that no ship of any nationality was to leave the harbours; any attempt would be prevented by whatever means were necessary. The Dutch were prisoners in their own country.

The occupation of Holland lasted just under five years. The hardships endured by the people of the Netherlands increased from year to year. At first, at least on the surface, the situation was not too greatly altered from pre-war days. Newspapers were published daily and, in fact, a glance at Amsterdam's most popular newspaper, *De Telegraaf*, ·will hardly reveal any difference from the week before the war compared with the day after capitulation, except for the prominently displayed exchange rate between the Reichsmark and the Dutch guilder.

The changes in Dutch life came more slowly and more subtly. Newspapers

145

Dutch women in traditional dress stroll past a lonely German on guard duty

Early attempts at friendliness meet with limited success

...osed down one by one. Rationing, ...hich had come into effect during the ...obilization in 1939, continued and ...adually became more stringent, ...pecially for goods which Holland had ...ormally received from her colonies, ...ch as coffee, rice, chocolate, sugar ...d tea. In almost every Dutch town ...ermans in uniform were about. ...rmed German soldiers were always ...evidence at railway stations, guard-...g against possible sabotage. Passen-...r trains became less frequent, par-...cularly after the invasion of Russia ...1941, since rolling stock was needed ...r the transport of troops and goods ...the Eastern Front. Dutch towns, ...used to the sight of non-Europeans, ...on became aware of the presence of ...sian troops, who had 'volunteered' to ...in units of the Waffen-SS; Indians, ...khs, Mongoloid types of uncertain

nationality. The atmosphere, above all, had changed. Some things were simply not discussed. Jews, almost from the first, were issued yellow stars of David which they were forced to display on their outer clothing. Quiet sympathy from many Dutchmen was evident for their Jewish countrymen, and a few openly helped them. Open persecution was confined to signs quickly erected in cafés, indicating that Jews were not allowed inside; these signs appeared on park benches and in many public places, but mass transportation of Jews to concentration camps did not begin in earnest until 1943.

The Germans had been given a quite definite briefing about how to treat this conquered state. Inasmuch as the Dutch were considered by the Nazis almost as good as the Germans themselves – were it not for cruel fate and the vicissitudes of history the Dutch might have been lucky enough to have

been Germans all along – and since they were unquestionably Germanic in language and race as defined by the Nazis, they were to be treated well. In the main, at first, they were. German soldiers tried to be kind, but this kindness was rather ungraciously received. The Dutch did not view themselves as the Wehrmacht high command did. The Dutch were a proud and independent nation, which had fought for its independence against many foreign invaders and the Germans, however well they viewed the Dutch, were placed by all but members of the NSB in the same category. Many German soldiers in the army of occupation did not understand what they considered to be ingratitude on the part of the Netherlanders, and within a few months' time the gap between conqueror and vanquished, which the Nazis hoped to narrow, in fact widened.

Before the war many Dutch who were not NSB members had some sympathy for Hitler. After all, he gave people work while there was still widespread unemployment and devaluation in Holland. But once the invasion had taken place, this sympathy melted away. There were many Dutch who opportunistically supported Germany; 50,000 actually joined the Waffen SS, and others worked as spies for the Gestapo. But the vast majority of Netherlanders resented the destruction of one of their greatest cities and the occupation with varying degrees of bitterness. Some, living in hopes of Allied victory, went through life as before though with a quiet desperation and shame. A few worked against Germany underground. But, contrary to popular belief today, there were few who rose against the invader until the dock strike in Amsterdam in late 1942, almost two years after the conquest. The Germans, of course, began to take over, one after another, important

A number of citizens, mostly pre-war NSB members, actively supported the new regime and welcomed the Germans

151

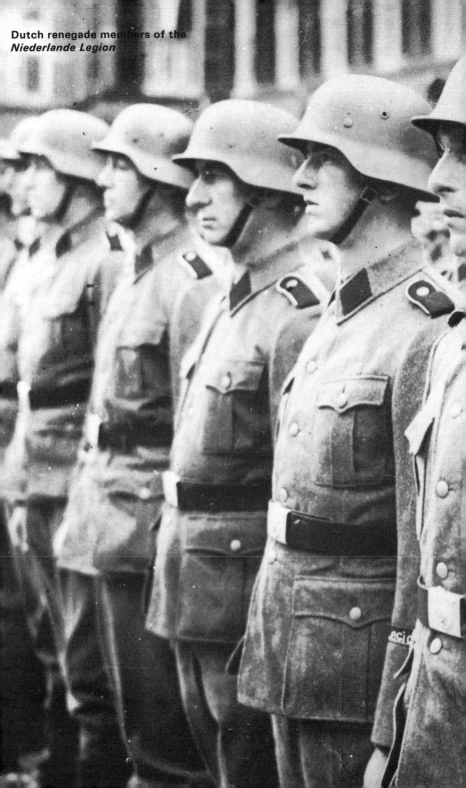

Dutch renegade members of the
Niederlande Legion

functions within what was left of the Dutch state. From key posts in the police down to even the stationmaster at every railway station 'safe' Dutchmen, and more often Germans themselves, were placed in charge. As the shock of defeat began to sink slowly into the consciousness of the Netherlands, just as slowly, but inexorably, a resistance, an underground, began to take shape.

On the walls of Dutch towns proclamations appeared indicating that someone in that town had been shot the day before, or that some people had been taken hostage, because a German soldier had been fired upon or killed. These attempts to cow the Dutch into submission proved counterproductive. As each patriot was taken to be shot, Dutch resistance stiffened. If few joined in active resistance – after all, as clothing and food became increasingly scarce, most people were concerned about their families first and foremost – resentment grew so that, by 1943, no German soldier dared

walk alone at night through even a Dutch village without his hand on his gun and a compatriot by his side.

A curious return to old Dutch habits of previous centuries began to take place which acted as a spur to the revival of nationalistic sentiment. For example, it became fashionable to wear a hand-knitted sweater made from irregularly homespun sheep's wool undyed and unbleached.

As food became scarcer, resentment against the ersatz German substitutes and the army of occupation began to show among the middle classes, which had been used to an abundance of food of all descriptions. As bread became harder to get and poorer in quality many turned to the black market for food, and others began to purchase wheat surreptitiously, reducing it to a coarse flour in their coffee grinders. The bread baked from this material in their ovens proved better than that which the baker, deprived of good wheat and flour, could produce.

Radio Oranje, the Dutch broadcast-

Above left: A German loudspeaker van delivers instructions to Dutch citizens.
Above: Polish troops liberate Breda and receive a spontaneous welcome. *Below:*
Messages of welcome proliferate on the flanks of this Polish tank as it progresses
through liberated Holland

The Allied food drops were more than welcome to the half-starved Dutch

ing service operating from Britain, was listened to avidly by many citizens despite the German interdictions against this activity. If one was caught listening to Radio Oranje or the BBC, one's radio was confiscated and prison was the likely next step. Nevertheless, news from the outside world was craved so desperately, and German radio and the German-controlled press were so distrusted, that any risk was worth the news of an Allied victory. As these victories became more commonplace, open resistance began to occur more frequently; and German control became more insistent and intrusive into private life with every setback in Africa or on the Eastern Front. The Jews began to be taken away. Some were hidden but many were caught, along with their Dutch friends. By D-Day food and coal were almost gone, and the Dutch were forced to endure the hunger-winter even when part of the country had been liberated at the end of 1944. Western Holland north of the rivers, including the great cities of The Hague, Amsterdam, Utrecht and what was left of Rotterdam, became a German enclave which was not liberated until the very end.

During the long and exceptionally cold winter of 1944-45 starvation was commonplace; thousands died of the cold and lack of food, and the middle-class was forced to sell its oriental carpets and antique furniture for wood and scraps of food or potatoes. Floorboards and furniture were burned for a few minutes of warmth. My family ate tulip bulbs, sugar beet and red cabbage every day for months. We were the lucky ones. My father had taken the precaution of buying up a truckload of cabbages in the autumn of 1944 and, although one became mightily sick of them by the time of liberation, we were properly grateful – many others lacked even the rudest necessities of existence. It was Holland's luck that that winter was the coldest and longest of the century. Trees did not begin to bud until May – when the war finally ended. The German occupation was more of a traumatic experience than we expected in 1940. It became a nightmare and a fight for survival which too many of my countrymen lost. The Netherlands paid the ultimate price for neutrality, a lack of preparedness and a lack of arms, which the short-sighted, throughout the 1930s, defended as keenly as those who defend neutrality and disarmament in Europe do now. It was a price no one who lived through it would be prepared to pay again. No Dutchmen will ever forget the food dropped by the Allies just before the German capitulation. Tins with biscuits, chocolates and bacon fell into the hands of the starving millions. Our bodies, unused to this plenty, reacted violently when these rations were wolfed down.

Rotterdam has risen again from the ashes of 1940. The Europoort is the greatest harbour complex in the world, handling a staggering volume of ocean-going cargo – about 250 million tons a year. The skyline is dominated by the Euromast, a 570-foot observation tower from whose restaurant one can see miles of countryside beyond this burgeoning city. The traffic-free Lijnbaan provides an open promenade and shopping centre which has been copied all over Europe. When the city was rebuilt the typically narrow, winding streets of Holland were avoided, and broad highways capable of handling heavy traffic replaced the rubble. Trees and shrubs, parks and playgrounds abound, and a new underground system has been constructed (all the more remarkable since the city itself lies below sea level).

There is little left of the heart of what was Rotterdam; at least that the human eye can perceive. But the spirit of the city was not destroyed in the holocaust of 1940, and it was that spirit which rebuilt Rotterdam and which lives on in the hearts of the young Rotterdamers who never experienced the terror of May 1940.

The Euromast in the new, spacious Rotterdam